FAREWELL
TO THE
TWENTIETH CENTURY

A Compendium of the Absurd

PIERRE BERTON

Doubleday Canada Limited

Canadian Cataloguing in Publication Data

Berton, Pierre, 1920–
  Farewell to the 20th century : a compendium of the absurd

ISBN 0-385-25577-2

1. Popular culture – Canada – History – 20th century.
2. Popular culture – United States – History – 20th century.
3. Canada – Social life and customs – 20th century. 4. United States – Social life and customs – 20th century. I. Title.

HN103.5.B47 1996   306'.0971'0904   C96-930531-1

Jacket photograph by Denise Grant
Jacket design by Andrew Smith
Text design by Heidy Lawrance Associates
Printed and bound in the USA

Published in Canada by
Doubleday Canada Limited
105 Bond Street
Toronto, Ontario
M5B 1Y3

Contents

AN OPEN LETTER TO MY GRANDCHILDREN

This is your book. I've put it together so you can bone up on the Olden Days, as you call my time. It is a sober book about subjects that we all took very, very seriously. If, occasionally, a note of satire creeps into the text, I ask you to ignore it. Please try not to laugh at matters that concerned your elders. Sure, they may have been trivial, but they didn't seem so at the time.

Take, for instance, the Cold War. We believed that because of the Cold War, the world was going to blow up. We actually built bomb shelters in the basements of our fashionable split-level homes, or in our back gardens, in which to cower when the Cold War grew hot. Every bomb shelter came complete with a twenty-gauge shotgun to keep the neighbours out. In the Olden Days it was every man for himself—every woman, too, but we didn't mention *them*. All this came under the heading of "deterrence," and that applied to nations as well as to families.

In my century, everybody was concerned about spies. We knew there were spies everywhere because of all the spy novels and spy movies. There were so many spy novels that everybody, including the Russians and the Tasmanians, was convinced there was a spy in every rain barrel. The great thing about spies was that they got the best-looking, sexiest women. We were all in favour of that, except for a small band of plain-looking, unsexy women who formed organizations to stop all spy novels and movies containing sexy women—a laudable effort abetted by a man named Gorbachev, who stopped the Cold War dead. You don't need to know about him; he's toast. So are the bomb shelters and the ultra-modern split-level houses, which have since been replaced by monster homes.

One of the great inventions of my century was moon travel. People kept saying things like, "Well, if they can put a man on the Moon, you'd think they could invent a pop-up toaster that doesn't char the bread, or maybe instant coffee that doesn't taste like bilgewater." Or they said, "If they can put a man on the Moon, how come they can't find a cheap way to get us there for a holiday?"

The people who said that figured a non-stop trip to the Moon would be a lot easier on the nerves than the limousine ride to the airport, and the tedious wait in the lounge, and the frustrating hiatus at the baggage carousel, which were all a feature of supersonic air travel. A great film director made rocketing to the Moon look as easy as pecan pie. We all figured we'd have a moon service by 2001, but it turned out that the flight was going to be delayed owing to some small technical problems—

such as designing a space bus that would hold more than three people.

Actually, the Moon was always old hat, compared to Mars. We all realized that Mars was a sophisticated planet, criss-crossed with canals that made the St. Lawrence Seaway look like a brook. And the Martians! Sooner or later, we knew, they were going to land and blast us all. Or maybe they were in town already, cunningly disguised as hippies. How could you tell?

The problem was that a few spoilsports at Cape Kennedy sent a probe to Mars and discovered that someone had filled in all the canals and there wasn't a Martian in sight. Either they'd migrated or we'd been had. Fortunately, we had a back-up position. We simply turned the Martians into aliens with the same colour: green. Like the Martians, they, too, arrived in saucer-shaped spaceships. From time to time they kidnapped a few Earthlings for scientific observation. We know it's true and not only because of the movies. A good many politically correct witnesses are around, eager to appear on the talk shows and recount their experiences. The fiction writers, deprived of spies, are delighted.

After we ran out of spies we got something even better. We got terrorists. Terrorists were everywhere, bombing buildings, hijacking airplanes, knocking off heads of state, lurking outside every restaurant. The people who had made small fortunes writing about spies immediately switched to terrorist stories. Every cinema ran a terrorist movie at least once a month. Actually, some of these so-called terrorists were teenaged punks whose only cause was stealing women's handbags and plugging milk-store proprietors with easily available guns, while engaging in substance abuse. By the end of the century they were such a nuisance that many people, including politicians, urged that they should be done away with, preferably live (if that's the right expression), on TV.

Ah, television! Moving pictures in a little box in the living room. Sooner or later, during my century, every single man, woman, child, and dog—especially the kooky ones—was given their fifteen minutes on television. Mostly they were interviewed by a sycophantic person who asked all the proper questions (usually supplied by the guest) but who rarely listened to the answers.

Those were the days when morticians tried to pretend their customers weren't defunct but merely sleeping in a beautifully cushioned casket; when people worried about the population explosion, but flinched at advertisements for condoms; when tobacco was illegal even if it killed you, but marijuana, which killed nobody, was *verboten*; when everything was "instant," from opinions to coffee, and the most terrifying phrase, from a father's point of view, was "easy to assemble."

The great buzz phrases in my century were the "hard sell" and the "rat race." The hard sell was a phrase invented by advertising men of the time who couldn't do anything softly. The hard sell was used to convince consumers that one single magic product—a new kind of brassière, a specially formulated soap—could change your personality. One agency tried its best to convince men that a little dab of hair cream would instantly make them irresistible to the opposite sex. The ad men also invented the rat race, and, indeed, became its chief victims, for they were all Type-A personalities, a phrase that entered the lexicon in the 1970s to describe those high-strung males who were constantly looking at their watches and were clearly candidates for a heart attack. The rat race was fuelled by greed and envy— the desire to be the first on one's block to flaunt the latest gimmick, whether it be a new-style funeral or a personalized Christmas card.

Horrible, isn't it? Well, there's more. Can you believe that there was a period (I lived through it) when the most popular singer on radio was a chipmunk? I wonder if things will improve in your century. How will the people of the future contemplate the absurdities of our time? Will some future archaeologist dig up an old pop bottle and puzzle over its significance? Will it take longer than ever to reach the airport from your domicile? Sometimes I try to project myself into the future and look backward to try to figure out if life will get even crazier after the turn of the century. In that sense I guess I'm a "futurist." That's the big buzzword now. But have the futurists got it right?

Don't laugh. Are things really better out there in the future? Is there a Hilton on the Moon? Do you have such a thing as a divorce ceremony? Do they execute criminals on TV? What's the new, approved name for "funeral director"? Have they finally banned cigarettes, or is it the other way round: can you buy a pack of Acapulco Gold at your nearest Mom and Pop store? What's the latest promotional gimmick? Or have the soap companies gone back to the free towel? Has radio come up with a slogan to replace The Sound That's New?

Have they actually succeeded in decommercializing Christmas? Has the population explosion made it illegal to have a child?

You tell me about the future. After all, you live there. I'm still saying goodbye to the past.

One

FABLES FOR OUR TIME

Never trust the artist. Trust the tale ...
D. H. Lawrence

A COLD WAR SPY STORY

Of all the spies in the old Soviet secret service, none was more skilled in the delicate job of filching blueprints than Vasili Gregorovitch Andreofsky, better known as Secret Agent X-9. And so when he arrived suddenly at Moscow airport, direct from North America, there was a flurry of excitement at the Kremlin.

His superiors waited breathlessly behind the great glass-topped desk at Intelligence H.Q. while X-9 dipped into that familiar bulging briefcase and unrolled a vast sheet of paper.

"Gentlemen," he said, his voice trembling, "I believe this to be the most important set of plans ever smuggled out of any Western nation."

The three top intelligence chiefs examined the complicated diagrams carefully. Finally one spoke:

"What are they?"

"They are so immensely complicated," X-9 replied, "that even my practised eye has not been able to master them. I believe them to be connected with secret installations near Washington. A cursory glance at Step Four will give you some idea of their incredible intricacy:

Assemble Lift No. 5

Take guide with dimble facing upward and 4 tabs through slots over lift handle in back of housing and bend 4 tabs on printed side flat. See Figs 1, 2 , and 3.

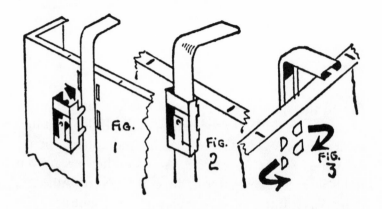

"What's a dimble?" asked the chief consulting engineer, who had been hastily summoned.

"Don't *you* know?" asked an intelligence chief. "Then it's obviously in code. I'd guess that Cipher would crack it in a couple of months."

"Granting that," a second intelligence chief asked, "how long do you engineers think it might take to assemble a working model?"

"The parts can be made easily," the engineer replied. "It's putting the thing together that is going to be complicated. Given unlimited money and labour, we could launch a crash program that might break the back of it in, say, six months."

The order was given at once. Work on the interplanetary ballistic missile came to a dead stop as men, material, and brains were seconded for the task.

The program almost bogged down during the third month because of difficulties with Step 6:

Assemble items 9 and 10.
Follow Step No. 2. See Fig A. Take Part No. 11 and bend into U-shape. Print Outside. See Fig. B. Now assemble housing to Base No. 1. See Fig. C. Then place assembled Lift No. 9 and 10 in Housing. See Fig. D.

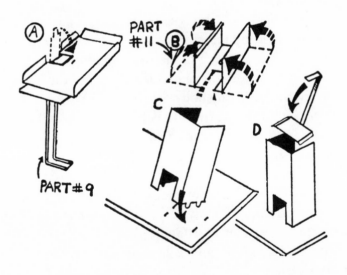

A top USSR physicist, detached from the Man-in-Space Program, laboured ninety-six hours without sleep and managed to crack Step 6.

Even more difficulty was encountered with Step 10.

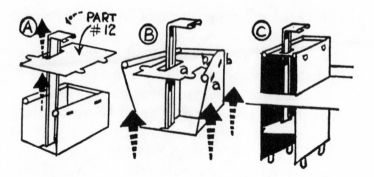

The Nobel Prize winners had to be committed to sanitariums on the Black Sea, suffering from nervous exhaustion trying to bend lugs A and B into the appropriate slots.

In spite of the crash program, the assembly job was not completed by target date, and it was not until late August that a working model was finally put together and brought before the Supreme Council of the Soviets.

"What is it?" somebody asked.

"We just don't know," the chief engineer acknowledged. "I suggest we get an expert from America here at once."

A special cable was dispatched and a few days later a scientific attaché from the Soviet consular office in Ottawa arrived, a highly respected technician and former close friend of Igor Gouzenko. He took one look at the metal model and a look of pure respect crept into his eyes.

"How on earth did you manage to get it together?" he asked. "I've been trying since Christmas Eve."

"What is it?" they cried.

"Deluxe Toy Service Station with mechanical lift,"

the attaché said promptly. "Eaton's winter catalogue, page 52. We bought one for little Sergei last Yuletide." He paused for a moment and a look of horror crossed his face. "In the catalogue," he said, "the phrase is: *easily assembled.*"

And he sat down with his head in his hands while his big frame shook with sobs at the memory of it all.

ANNALS OF SCIENTIFIC ADVANCE

Frankie and Johnny

Frankie and Johnny were lovers; make no mistake about that; and, Lordy, how they could love.

Johnny didn't mind that Frankie was insanely jealous. He felt kind of flattered that she cared so much, though it bothered him that sometimes she thought he was two-timing her. He wasn't. He was as true as the stars above. Still, he made it a habit to come home directly from work so she wouldn't think he was out with a bimbo.

On this particular day, he hurried home, stopping only to pick up a copy of *Vanity Fair*, which often contained revealing stories about Hollywood notables, hidden among the perfume ads.

Frankie was waiting for him on the doorstep, but when he embraced her, she turned on him.

"Who is she?" she shrieked. Johnny was baffled. "I

can smell her perfume on you," Frankie screamed. When Johnny tried to reason with her, she pulled out a nickel-plated revolver. Rooti-toot-toot, three times she shoot, and her Johnny-man fell dead.

As he fell, the offending magazine, redolent of all those perfume ads, dropped from his fingers.

Lucille LeSeur

When Lucille LeSeur was seven, her teacher knew she was destined to be a great actress. Her high school drama teacher predicted she'd become a Hollywood star. At the Royal Academy of Dramatic Arts they said she was a second Vivien Leigh. Her voice was crystal clear, her style direct and positive, her accent mid-Atlantic and unaffected. There was a no-nonsense quality about her delivery.

A vast international organization sought her out. They held 100 auditions. She won hands down. They suggested she adopt a similar name, like Joan Crawford, to fit the dialogue they gave her; but being a woman of integrity, she refused.

Now, when she says, "Hang up, and try your call again; if you need assistance, dial your operator," she knows she has the largest audience in the country.

Nick the Bellboy

When young Nick Charles was hired as bellboy by the fabulously elegant Helmsbury hotel chain, he was in seventh heaven. Fiercely ambitious, he was determined to rise to the top and become the greatest hotelier in the world before going to jail for tax evasion. No task was too menial for him, no job too difficult. So when Irving Zolf on the front desk told him a light bulb needed changing in the men's room on the convention floor, he sprang into action.

Since it was clearly identified as a "washroom," young Nick decided to first wash his hands, as his mother had always advised him.

He searched about for a roller towel, but there was no roller towel.

He looked around for a paper towel dispenser, but there was no such device.

At last he spotted one of the new handy-dandy hot-air hand dryers. He pressed the button, tried to shake the excess water from his hands as instructed, and waited … and waited … and waited for his hands to dry. Alas, they stayed damp.

So Nick, ever eager to get the job done, removed the dead bulb with damp hands, and before replacing it, stuck his finger in the socket to get rid of dead moths.

A coroner's jury returned a verdict of death by misadventure. "Didn't he know water conducts electricity?" a juror asked. "Why didn't he dry his hands?"

But we, who have tried this modern device, know why, don't we?

Ralph Rackstraw

"You can always reach me at this number, day or night," Ralph Rackstraw's cardiologist told him after his attack.

"Remember, if you feel the slightest chest pain, call me at once. Every minute may count."

One June 11, 1992, while sitting at his desk in McLemore's Hay & Feed, Ralph felt a sharp, stabbing pain, reached for the phone, and dialled the magic number.

A recorded voice told him that the number he had dialled was a long-distance number and he must use the area code. He dialled again, feeling his heart thump alarmingly, and another voice (or was it the same voice?) told him it was not a long-distance call.

His doctor had told him that whatever happened, he must stay calm. But now, as beads of sweat stood out on his brow, he felt a sense of fury and frustration. His heart thumped wildly.

He dialled again, and a voice told him, "The number you have reached is not in service. Please hang up and try your call again."

Something snapped inside him. The phone dropped from his nerveless fingers. As he slumped forward he continued to hear, over and over, a calm, unaccented voice urging him to dial the operator for assistance. Thus, the last words he ever heard were those of Lucille LeSeur.

SAM SYLVESTER'S GREAT DETERRENT

When Freddy Creel went up to Sam Sylvester's place for dinner, he knew he would be exposed to Sam's collection of Things. Sam was a great collector. He collected old warming pans, ancient cigar cutters, candle moulds, butter paddles, even moustache cups.

This time he had collected himself a handsome bronze cannon, Napoleonic period. He had it out on his front porch, nicely shined and pointed directly across at the home of his neighbours, the Finchleys.

"How d'you like this baby?" Sam asked, patting the cannon, and Freddy mumbled something appropriate.

"Course, it takes a lot of upkeep, especially after it's been fired," Sam said.

"Fired?" asked Freddy. He had been looking across at the Finchley's house. There seemed to be several rather ugly holes in the outer walls and two or three ragged breaks in the roof line.

"Needs cleaning every time," said Sam. "Then, of

course, the balls are quite expensive, but we try to reuse the ones that land over here."

He had scarcely finished speaking when there was a window-rattling roar and a flash from the direction of the Finchleys. A cannon ball tore through a corner of the dining room and landed with a splash in a steaming tureen that Mrs. Sylvester had just set out.

"Oh Sam!" said Mrs. Sylvester. "There goes our soup, and me spending the whole morning on it."

"By george, a lucky hit!" cried Sam Sylvester. "Well, he won't get away with that! What does he think we're made of over here, anyway?"

He picked up a ball from a handy pile and stuffed it down the cannon's gaping mouth.

"Get their satellite dish, Sam!" cried Mrs. Sylvester, running for the matches. "Slice it off. You know how furious Ab Finchley gets when he can't bring in Atlanta."

"Watch this now, Fred," Sam said, touching off the fuse. The cannon spoke, shaking the porch, and a moment later the Finchleys' dish was a twisted mass.

"Last week we knocked out their automatic dishwasher and poor Finchley has had to wipe the dishes every night since," said Sam, glowing with satisfaction. "Now I'm after their deep-freeze. If I can only find where it is, I'll lay one in there and finish off his stock of TV dinners for good and all."

"That's the trouble: we don't know where they keep things," said Mrs. Sylvester. "Oh, they're secretive, I can tell you. You never saw such a family!"

"Better move the hi-fi again, Mother," said Sam. "You never know."

Mrs. Sylvester rolled the hi-fi cabinet off down the hall and into a closet. Mere seconds later a cannon ball crashed through the roof and dropped neatly into the empty corner, crushing a Wedgwood ashtray and the Sylvesters' cat in the process.

"By heaven, he's gone too far!" shouted Sam Sylvester, shoving another ball down his cannon's mouth. "Firing at legitimate targets is one thing, but when you kill defenceless cats, that's too much." And, blind with rage, he fired recklessly in the general direction of the Finchleys' home. The ball bounced harmlessly off the chimney.

"He's got it reinforced with steel girders," said Sam. "Must have cost him a pretty penny; no wonder they never can go out nights. Well, we're just going to have to bring in heavier guns!"

"How did it all start?"

"I guess it began when their kid started firing off his BB gun around here," Sam said. "I warned Finchley we couldn't have that, but it kept on, so I got this shotgun out just to scare him. One day I figured I'd let him have a blast. Sort of pepper his fence a bit to prevent things going too far. Finchley got mad and drilled a hole in my picture window with a .22 slug. That's when I bought this cannon. I figured when he saw that thing sitting on the porch he'd quit, and he did, too, for a while. It really shook him.

"Then one day I'm coming home and I see this other cannon on Finchley's porch. He began sneering at me, saying if I so much as dared to send a whiff of grape across his front lawn, he'd smash up my barbecue. Well, a man can take just so many insults and then he's got to act. I tell you, since then I've given it to him hot and heavy every night after work.

"Who's that at the door?" cried Sam Sylvester, whirling about, a look of dark suspicion on his face.

"Just the paper boy come to collect," said Mrs. Sylvester.

"Oh no it's not!" cried Sam, rushing to the door and seizing a small boy by the nape of the neck. "Collection day is Saturday! This is one of those little sneaks sent over by the Finchleys to find out where we keep the Bendix. I knew he had inside information!"

He thrust the terrified child into a closet and locked the door.

"Couple of hours in the dark without supper and he'll be ready to tell us everything," said Sam. "I just bet he knows the new layout of their family room. I'd dearly like to get their spin-dry."

As he spoke, another cannon ball tore a great piece out of his fireplace.

"Supper, Sam!" cried Mrs. Sylvester.

"Just one more shot, lover," said Sam. "I think I can crack his stone planting box with this one. You know how he prides those begonias."

"Well, hurry it up, then," said Mrs. Sylvester. "The stew's getting cold. Sorry we can't offer you anything fancy," she said, turning to Freddy, "but the house repairs have been particularly heavy this month. And then there are the gunpowder bills. It mounts up, you know."

Freddy Creel nodded sympathetically, wincing only slightly as the cannon roared again.

Sam Sylvester came to the table rubbing his hands in satisfaction.

"Any cold beer, hon?" he asked. "That's warm work."

"Oh, Sam," said Mrs. Sylvester. "I've just this minute sandbagged the fridge for the night. Do you mind?"

"Guess not," said Sam Sylvester. "After all, it's only temporary. Tomorrow I'm going straight to the armourer's. He's got a big one in the window, powerful enough to blast Ab Finchley's place right off the map. When he sees that on my porch he'll think twice before he threatens me again!"

As he spoke, Freddy Creel heard once more the now-familiar thunder of a cannon, followed by the harsh rattle of grapeshot striking the Sylvesters' Edsel broadside, and destroying the beautiful Simonized finish.

A TWENTIETH-CENTURY CONFESSION
(A found document)

My name is Harry J. Grimm, and this is my confession. I make it without cajolery or threat of duress, neither for private recompense nor hope of gain, nor in the interests of cheap sensationalism or personal publicity, but simply in the honest belief that some other poor soul, on reading these words, may—before it is too late—escape the fate that dooms me. If one single person is helped by this testimony, then my story will not have been told in vain.

It all began seventeen years ago when I sent my first Christmas card. I was a mere slip of a youth at the time and I purchased, for a nickel, a comic greeting card with Mickey Mouse on it dressed as Santa Claus. I sent it to a friend of mine, about four days before Christmas.

That Christmas Eve, a special-delivery letter arrived containing a Christmas card for me from my friend. It was worth at least fifteen cents and it made me feel cheap.

That was when I began my Christmas List. It contained

only one name, but the next year after I sent four more Christmas cards, the list increased to five. You see, all those people sent cards to me immediately.

On the third Christmas I sent cards to all the people who had sent me cards—a total of now twenty-seven—but to my horror received back thirty-three. Five had sent me cards whom I hadn't sent cards to. I rushed out, bought some rather soiled cards, and sent them off posthaste.

The following year, to prevent this embarrassment, I sent out fifty-four Christmas cards to everybody I could think of. But on Christmas Eve I discovered I had received sixty-two cards.

I cross-checked my list immediately and a cold shiver ran down my spine. Some of the people I had sent cards to had *not* sent cards to me! This meant, and I still shudder at the memory of it, that I had got *more* than eight cards from people I had not sent cards to.

All that night, when not a creature was stirring, not even a mouse, I carefully checked my list. The stores were closed on Christmas Day and I was in a blind panic. The following day I found one drugstore open and persuaded the pharmacist to bootleg fourteen cards to me.

I signed these cards and added effusive messages, then dated them all December 21. On most of them I put in mocking little notes about the inefficiency of the postal service at Christmas time.

The following year I got married. My wife brought, with her dowry, a careful Christmas-card list of her own, and we spent many carefree evenings amalgamating the two.

That year we sent out 134 cards. We received back 157 cards, many of which did not cross-check. But I had prepared myself for such emergencies, having bought extra cards, all enveloped and ready to dispatch with lightning speed.

The next year all went reasonably well, although after Christmas I was deluged with an avalanche of cards from people who had received cards from me but hadn't sent me a card.

The following year my wife suggested that we get cards with our names stamped in gold. After a lightning calculation and a careful cross-examination of the amalgamated and updated Christmas-card list, I ordered 225 cards. They were a standard model, showing pink and white poinsettias on a solid-gold background with a blue lining and this message:

Just a note from us to you
And a message fine and true
At this happy Christmas season
You'll never find us blue!

THE GRIMMS
"THE PINES"
ROSLYN AVE.

Unfortunately, the greeting-card company got the name wrong and it came out:

THE PINES
"THE GRIMMS"
ROSLYN AVE.

The cards had to be redone, of course, and this, together with the fact that my wife was now insisting on writing lengthy personal notes in each of them, meant that they got out very late.

As a result a lot of people who were on our list because they got cards from us the year before but hadn't planned to send *us* cards because we hadn't sent *them* cards received our cards so late in the season that it was difficult for them to get more cards to send us in time for Christmas.

Our list, in the next three years, rose to 517.

By this time we had two children, and my wife was now suggesting that their pictures ought to be on the Christmas cards. She said they ought to have photographs of the heads, with little bodies drawn on.

I spent about a week dealing with artists and photographers that year. The inscription read:

> *At this season of the year*
> *When we're feeling real sincere*
> *We wish "wealth" and lots of health*
> *To all those that we hold dear.*
> *Vina   Madge   Delice   Harry   &   Jock*
> (Jock is our dog.)

That year we received 612 Christmas cards and had to go into a second printing.

Yet that year's seems like child's play compared to what I now face.

The entire fall months from October onward are now devoted to the preparation of Christmas cards; I take a leave of absence from my job. My staff of trained accountants checks and cross-checks the gargantuan master list, which I keep in filing cabinets in a special vault. Names are added and deleted in a matter of moments and each new card is automatically cross-indexed by a special IBM machine designed for the purpose.

In the drafting room skilled artists work on this year's card while others submit roughs of future cards. Across the patio, my hack writers polish and hone the words of this year's greeting. Photographers are busy, as I write, capturing "cute" poses of my newest children.

This is the end of my story, but the tragedy is that it has no end. Each year the crushing burden increases, but I cannot see any solution.

You who read heed my folly.

THE TYPE-A PERSONALITY:
A case study

"Goddammit!" he cried, "are you coming or aren't you? We haven't much time."

He had half risen from his restaurant seat, having called for and signed the check, but she didn't budge.

"What's the panic!" she said placidly. "There's lots of time."

"The movie starts in exactly fourteen minutes," he told her. "We have to get out of here, get the car, drive to the theatre, park the car, and buy the tickets. You think that's plenty of time?"

"It's just down the street," she said. "And I haven't quite finished my coffee."

She picked up the cup, gave it half a turn, raised it briefly to her lips, then set it down again. As far as he could divine, the only coffee left was a kind of brown stain at the bottom. Since she couldn't sip it, she licked at it.

Out of the corner of his eye he caught a movement

at the front of the restaurant: terrorists with stocking masks coming through the door, cradling in their arms black objects which he recognized from the movies as Uzis, or maybe Oozies.

She was still examining the coffee cup when he leaped for her, flung her over his shoulder, and plunged towards the kitchen door.

"What the hell are you doing?" she screamed. "I haven't finished my coffee!"

Through the swinging doors, past an army of chefs and sous chefs, the rattle of machine-guns in the background and a waiter struggling behind him, his face streaming blood.

"Oh my God!" she cried. "Oh my God!"

He threw her into the car, slammed the door, and hurtled out of the parking lot.

"Oh my God!" she said again.

"We've got exactly nine minutes before the feature starts," he told her. "We'll just about make it."

"Come *on!*" he was saying. "The last tender leaves the dock in less than five minutes."

"What's the panic?" she asked him. "We're practically there and I want to pick up one of these cute straw hats the natives make."

"There isn't time," he shouted. "They won't wait. The gangplank goes up the moment the tender reaches the ship. They told us that, remember?"

"There's lots of time," she said. "I can see the tender down by the jetty. People are still climbing aboard."

It was then he noticed the rumbling beneath his feet,

and looking upward at the mountain behind them, he saw the pillar of smoke trickling from the summit thicken and expand. It was then he remembered what the taxi driver had said on the shore excursion: "Fire god heap angry!"

He seized her by the hair, threw her over his shoulder, and dashed for the jetty. The rumbling grew louder. Just as he reached the tender somebody shouted, "Cast off!" He threw her into the boat and leaped in after her as it headed out into the water. A moment later the mountain exploded and a fog of hot ash sizzled into the sea around them.

He heaved a sigh of relief as the tender reached the gangway. "Thank God we're on the second sitting," he said. "We can linger over dessert."

He preferred a bulkhead seat on the aisle. That way he could be the first off the aircraft the moment it came to a full stop outside the terminal building.

"Come *on!*" he cried. "Let's move."

"What's the panic?" she asked. "They haven't even opened the doors."

"You know damn well there's only a few taxis at this cockamamie airport," he told her. "If you don't get off and grab one first, you're stuck waiting for half an hour."

To his frustration, she hadn't even undone her seatbelt. As he fiddled with it he noticed a small, dark man furtively move up the aisle ahead of everybody and then, as the doors opened, rush pell-mell down the steps. He realized: *He's purposely left his briefcase behind!*

He seized her by the collar and literally threw her down the steps.

"*Run!*" he cried, as they tumbled to the bottom. "Run for your life!"

The little man was ahead of them as they dashed towards the terminal. The explosion came a moment later—human screams, mingled with the sounds of jagged metal clanging on the tarmac all around them.

"Thank God!" he said as they dashed through. "There's one taxi left. We won't have to hang around."

The strange little man, he noticed, had taken the other.

"We'd better go," he told her. "Remember they told us we have to be at the airport an hour ahead."

"What's the panic?" she said. "There's plenty of time and I haven't quite finished my coffee. You always do this! You rush off like a madman, forgetting half your stuff, and then we spend an hour hanging around the airport."

"For God's sake," he told her. "You know how bad the traffic is in the morning. If we leave right now we'll just barely make it."

She continued to sip her coffee placidly. He drummed his fingers on the table, then suddenly made his decision.

"You do what you want," he told her. "I'm going out to get a taxi right now. You can come or not as you like."

He picked up his suitcase and plunged out the front door. She heard the scream of brakes, the sound of the crash, the tinkling of broken metal on the pavement.

The policeman was appropriately gloomy. "I'm afraid there's been a bad accident, Ma'am," he said. "We think it's your husband. I'm afraid we'll need you to identify the body."

She did not move.

"Ma'am," he said. "Are you coming?"

"In a minute," she told him. "What's the panic? I haven't quite finished my coffee."

DIAMONDS AREN'T FOREVER

I wonder if anybody now remembers the name of Homer Skrim, that brooding shadow of a man who, in the words of Walter Cronkite, "left his brief, blurred imprint on the paving blocks of history, then melted quietly away."

They still remember him in the business world, of course—with a shudder. (There's a bit of stock-market strategy called a Skrim.) And in the fever-ridden bush country of Tanganyika his name is legend.

The "why" of Skrim is still something of a mystery, though a score of reporters once tried to unravel it. Certainly they got no help from the man himself, walled off in his shack in that arid African valley. He was a mining engineer, that much is known. Indeed, for a time he taught geology at the University of Toronto. He is remembered there as a mild, inoffensive young instructor with no interests except his work and, of course, his girl. You may remember she came in for some notoriety at the time. Thelma Hunt—does that ring a bell?

She was one of his students, and by all accounts her family was incredibly wealthy. (Banks, life insurance, beer, private TV stations.) Skrim, of course, was penniless, but he managed to persuade Thelma to marry him.

It was the engagement party, apparently, that changed his life. He'd saved about $350 for furniture, but discovered at the last moment that Thelma was expecting a ring. In the circles in which she moved they wore them like medals. When their race-horse, Rabbit Face, came in last at Woodbine one year, Mrs. Hunt personally choked it to death. Know what she used? Her diamond ring! That's right: it was big enough to choke a horse.

So Skrim blew his furniture money on a ring. There was a rather swank party at the family mansion, but it was not a success. It must be remembered that $350 was a fortune for Skrim. He didn't understand why a cold hush fell across the assembly when he placed the ring on Thelma's finger. Several women fainted when they saw how small it was and had to be revived with Vichy water. Thelma looked as if she'd been struck across the face with a riding crop. Naturally, the engagement was broken off.

The incident embittered Skrim. He vanished for four years. We know now, of course, that he went to Africa on a cattle boat, got a grubstake from a merchant on the coast, and began to prospect along the veldt.

The general impression has been that his prospecting was aimless. It seems more probable, however, that every move was calculated. He went to Tanganyika because there were diamonds there. He brought every scrap of geological knowledge into play. I am quite certain that when Homer Skrim found the largest diamond mine in the world no flash of surprise crossed his face. It was exactly what he had been seeking.

It was six months before the news leaked out. There was a mild sensation and some speculation about how much the diamond syndicate would buy him out for. A truckload of reporters headed for Skrim's shack in the veldt. They never got past the barbed wire.

But the big sensation was to come. The trade began to hear murmurs that Skrim wouldn't sell. Then the real shock hit the world headlines: Skrim had turned up on a streetcorner in Johannesburg with a gunny sack full of rough diamonds, which he hawked for fifteen cents apiece.

He was stopped, of course. The preliminary charge of obstructing traffic was quite justified. The later charges of insanity couldn't be established because Skrim bolted and couldn't be found. It was too late anyway; the panic had started.

The business of selling diamonds in the street was only a gesture. Skrim was far better organized. His mine had been turning out thousands of diamonds, which his agents began to unload by the sackful to every dime store in the world.

Remember those crowds at Honest Ed's, pushing and screaming, when diamonds went on sale at 10 a.m., reduced to clear at two for a quarter? Why, in less than a month the bottom dropped out of the diamond market and Skrim was an overnight hero. He had made the richest stones in the world available to all. Editorials praised him; small towns raised monuments to him. Charwomen wore tiaras; panhandlers sported flashy 24-karat stickpins. Everyone was suddenly rich, or thought he was.

Looking back on it all, it's difficult to understand why nobody foresaw the outcome. The first hint came in small news stories: a bachelor assaulted by an insulted fiancée because he presented her with a cheap 40-karat engagement ring. Then a group calling itself the Associated Brides of Yesteryear sprang up. This organization, whose president was the former Thelma Hunt, pointed out that diamond rings, once symbolic of undying love, were now about as valuable as glass and as symbolic as ice cubes.

Editorials began to echo these sentiments. Skrim had robbed every woman who had owned a diamond ring, they cried; he was a jewel thief—a warped and distorted mind who had played a cruel trick on humanity. Mobs began to tear down his monuments.

By this time the public was weary of diamonds. The mad vogue for them passed as suddenly as it began. It was generally agreed that they were "common." The diamond became a symbol of everything that was cheap and tawdry, and it became a deadly insult to call a man a diamond in the rough. Soon the jewels were used exclusively for bicycle reflectors, stop signs, Christmas tree ornaments, and dolls' eyes.

Nobody knows who first suggested using emeralds for engagement rings, but the vogue was quickly established. A combine cornered the market early in the game and emeralds at once doubled in price. That made everybody feel secure. Today, emeralds are worth five times as much as they were in the days when the embittered Skrim was plodding across the veldt seeking revenge in diamonds. Today, as we know, every man is happy to impoverish himself in order that his fiancée may wear an emerald engagement ring.

And Homer Skrim? A forgotten man. He's still in Africa, I'm told. He didn't make a cent out of diamonds, of course; he didn't want to. He never did marry, either, though I hear he was engaged to a girl in Johannesburg. He had to break the whole thing off. Poor chap couldn't raise the price of an emerald ring.

THE ELBOW WORSHIPPERS:
A salutary report

I had an interesting talk last week with one of the world's best-known explorers and anthropologists, Professor Gulliver Grasmere, who had just returned from exploring the native civilizations of the Upper Amazon.

Professor Grasmere tells me that this jungle fastness is not entirely inhabited by untutored savages. In fact, he spent more than a year studying the little-known society of Snarfs (or, to give them their original German spelling, *Schnarffes*). There are some seventy-five thousand of these Snarfs living in small cities, towns, and villages in the inaccessible Grool, a mountain plateau that was, until the development of the long-range helicopter, entirely cut off from the world.

Professor Grasmere's studies have cast new light on the Snarf custom of elbow worship, a practice only sketchily referred to in earlier anthropological works. In this oddly gifted society—whose political sophistication is beyond dispute—the men seem to be totally obsessed not only with the female elbow but also with the fore-arm, the hand, and the fingers.

A woman appearing in public with her elbows undraped would be considered grossly indecent, and anyone daring to walk about freely with bare arms would be driven from the streets and, indeed, imprisoned.

Professor Grasmere, however, remains confused by the elbow mania since it is not really true that the feminine elbow is hidden for masculine eyes in Snarf society. In fact, a recent count made by the professor suggests that in spite of long-held taboos, there are now more Snarf elbows showing than there are Snarf elbows hidden.

For one thing, many of the most stylish gloves are worn so lightly that every detail of the arm is observable to the most casual eye. For another, it has become highly fashionable to affect semi-transparent gloves that leave little to the imagination. Again, on the beach and for evening wear, style-conscious Snarf women have fol-lowed the trend of partially rolling down their gloves to reveal about seven-eighths of their elbow.

Almost every Snarf publication for men now features detailed pictures of not one but dozens of undraped elbows, even a bit of the palm, though these have been the objects of recent attempts at censorship. Many the-atrical performances and native dances feature sugges-tive elbow and hand movements, and, again, the elbows are undraped. A book, if it is to attract attention, must feature on its cover a picture of a giant elbow. Classical paintings abound in naked elbows and are widely praised. And in the cheaper novelty shops, ashtrays and other bric-à-brac in the form of elbows enjoy a steady sale among the sophisticated males.

Thus, male Snarfs are literally surrounded by elbows; yet they continue to be excited by them. Even a wrinkled glove lying on a chair will cause sniggers and whispered comments. Indeed, younger Snarfs have been known to stage "glove raids" on female dormitories.

It is difficult to move down the main street of any Snarf settlement without encountering elbow symbols on every side; yet the sight of a quarter inch of naked elbow protruding from a worn glove will cause a near panic and give rise to write-ups in the newspapers.

A bizarre by-product of this elbow-directed society, Professor Grasmere reports, is the grotesque anatomical distortions it has caused. Women with enlarged elbow bones or particularly hefty forearms are much in demand, especially as entertainers. Professor Grasmere interviewed several of these pathetic creatures who, by virtue of muscle exercise and even surgical operation, had managed to increase the size of their elbows to the point where it became difficult to walk upright or perform simple feats of manual dexterity. They are looked on, he discovered, by both men and other women as near goddesses. Some of them, he reports, have to carry their arms in special slings for support, but this seems to make them all the more desirable.

Some years ago, certain women—disgraced in the eyes of their parents and friends by the physical accident of underdeveloped elbows—began to use padded gloves. These, the professor says, have now become an important commercial by-product of Snarf society and are, indeed, advertised openly.

Another curious aspect of the Snarf elbow mania is the rise of the so-called Health Groups who insist that the enforced draping of the lower arm is unhealthy and physically undesirable. These people meet in secluded spots—private farms, beaches, and forest glades—where they affect a costume consisting of a wool cloak that covers the wearer from head to foot but leaves the arms entirely bare from the elbow down. Many attempts have been made to prevent these societies from meeting, but the fact that health is the key motive has protected them from legal action. Many publish health magazines showing pictures of the undraped elbow, and these have a wide sale since the male Snarfs, apparently, are extremely interested in health.

Professor Grasmere has done considerable historical research into the Snarf past and it is his belief that there was a time when the very word "elbow" was taboo in polite society. This is no longer the case, since it is used in books, plays, and theatre advertising, and always gets a laugh when employed by a stand-up comedian in a joke.

The taboo still applies, however, for words dealing with the concealed parts of the lower arm, especially the fingers. These are rarely if ever mentioned in public either by name or reference. A storm of protest was engendered recently with the publication of a book of considerable literary quality because it dared to employ the five-letter word "thumb"—a term theretofore confined entirely to scrawls on back fences and washroom walls.

That this book has been distributed, however, indicates a breaking down of traditional Snarf taboos. Indeed, Professor Grasmere says he has reason to believe that the sight of a naked elbow in the Upper Amazon may soon become almost as familiar as, say, the sight of a naked bosom in our own culture.

THE WAITING ROOM

*Wesbrook Frayme, 32-year-old racing ace, was instant-
ly killed today when his scarlet Whirling-Arrow went
into a skid and exploded on the third turn at the
Whiffing trials. Frayme's young wife, Claire, had to be
given sedatives when told of the accident. She was late
arriving at the scene and thus missed seeing her husband's fatal crash. "I know he's somewhere up there
waiting for me," she sobbed as friends led her away.*

"**Y**our wife should be arriving on the next draft," the
cherub announced as he led Wesbrook Frayme
into the waiting room. "I'm sorry we're so crowded. In
the old days when Hell was operating, and before that
when we had Purgatory, we didn't have this problem."

"You mean you've closed up Hell?"

"Oh no," said the cherub. "*You* closed it up. You
refused to accept the fact of it, so it just withered away.
Here's your seat. Just be patient and wait."

I'm always waiting for my wife, thought Wesbrook Frayme as he tipped the cherub. He looked about him. Just like a waiting room on earth, he thought, except it was solid gold and the Muzak leaned heavily towards harp selections: they were playing the "Shall We Gather at the River" cha-cha.

"I wish these gold seats weren't quite so hard!" said a portly middle-aged gentleman, taking a place beside him.

"Well, you asked for them, you know," said the cherub, holding out his hand for a tip. "You wanted everything of solid gold and pearl, so you got it. We aim to please, you know. Thanks, reverend. Much obliged."

"Reverend?" asked Wesbrook Frayme.

"The Reverend Peter Frenshaw," said the gentleman. "Central Monetarian Church, Vancouver. Packed 'em in solid Sunday nights. I made predictions, you know. Not much scope for that here, I'm afraid. I can't understand them not having churches. Puzzling."

"I wish my wife would hurry up," said Wesbrook Frayme.

"Room for good missionary work here," said the Reverend Mr. Frenshaw. "All those Hindus, eh? Virgin territory."

"She never could be on time," said Frayme.

"Some women need discipline," said the minister. "My wife was a spoiled child when I married her, but I made her toe the line. I gave the orders. She liked it that way."

"Aren't you sorry you didn't treat her better?"

"I treated her fine. I was the boss. She liked that."

"Then why isn't *she* on time?" asked Frayme. "*You're* waiting, you know."

"It's the beastly bureaucratic system they're running here," replied Frenshaw. "They're disorganized."

"Time moves like lead up here," said Frayme impatiently. "You—cherub! When does the next draft arrive? We can't wait forever, you know."

"Why not?" asked the cherub, showing an old gentleman to the seat beside them. "You've *got* forever!"

"Don't be impertinent to your elders," said Frenshaw.

"Elders!" cried the cherub. "I like *that!* Why, I was up here when your ancestors were orangutans. I've been a bellhop since the beginning."

"You mean you saw Adam and Eve come through?" asked Frenshaw a little breathlessly.

"Don't recall nobody by *that* name," the cherub said. "But we had a lot of hairy ones right after we opened. Better behaved than the crowd we get at present, if you ask me. You new ones are so *impatient.* Take a cue from the old guy next to you. He's sound asleep!"

And indeed, the old gentleman was snoring loudly.

"It's just like Claire to be late," muttered Frayme.

"Claire?" said the Reverend Peter Frenshaw. "How odd! That's *my* wife's name. Claire Frayme Frenshaw."

"*Frayme!*" cried Wesbrook Frayme.

"Right. Name of her first husband. A reckless chap, killed in a car accident. He spoiled her terribly, but I soon set that straight. She preferred firmness. Why, my dear fellow, are you ill?"

"*I* am her first husband," said Wesbrook Frayme in a strangled voice.

"Good—good Earth!" cried Frenshaw. "What effrontery. This is most distressing."

"Distressing! You wife thief!"

"Oh, now, really. She's quite forgotten you, you know."

"Nonsense. We were married for five years."

"Ah," said the Reverend Mr. Frenshaw, "but *we* were married for twenty."

Wesbrook Frayme put down his harp. "Why, that's quite impossible," he said. "It can't have been that long. It seems like only a few days ago that I left her."

"Twenty years!" said Frenshaw emphatically. "Look at me: I'm old enough to be your father!"

Wesbrook Frayme looked about wildly for the cherub.

The cherub gave him a strange look. "You were just saying how slowly time passed up here," he said. "We do our best to make it flit by. Isn't that the way you wanted it? *Heavenly?*"

As he spoke there came a sound of trumpets and the great gates of the waiting room began to open. The two men edged forward expectantly.

"I've got the advantage of youth," said Wesbrook Frayme. "She'll choose me. I treated her like a princess."

"Women prefer maturity to callowness," said Frenshaw. "She'll choose me. I treated her like a father."

The two men pushed forward and then, when they saw her, they gasped and recoiled. For she was as old as time— old and wrinkled, brown and senile. And she did not even see them. She walked right up into the arms of the old gentleman who had been snoring on the bench beside them.

"Great scott!" said Frenshaw. "It didn't occur to me that she'd marry a third time."

"How quickly you came," said the old gentleman as the two went off, arm in arm.

"But why *him?*" asked Wesbrook Frayme.

"Perhaps he treated her as an equal," said the ubiquitous cherub, sliding up beside them.

"You know," said Frayme thoughtfully, "I never did find out the name of this place. What do you call it, anyway?"

"I don't know as it has a name anymore," said the cherub. "We used to call it Heaven, but since you abolished *that,* it's sort of a mixture. We aim to please, but when you try to run a compromise you do have your problems."

THE DAY THE MARTIAN LANDED

The flying saucer landed on Fred Foster's back lawn at three o'clock on a Saturday afternoon. Fred's oldest girl, Mona, answered the door. There was a little green man standing there; he had a bald head, bulbous eyes, huge ears, and a pair of antennas protruding from his forehead. He was wearing a goldfish bowl on his head. She recognized him at once as a Martian.

"Take me to your leader," said the newcomer politely.

"Hey, Pop!" Mona called. "There's a Martian at the back door wants to see you."

Fred Foster was sitting in his undershirt in the television room, watching the football on Channel 2. "Tell him we don't want any!" he called back. "Whatever it is, we got plenty!"

"He ain't selling nothing, Pop," Mona called back. "He's a *Martian*."

Fred Foster got up wearily. "They'll do anything to

get into the house," he said. "Last week they told me I'd won a free health course."

He glared at the Martian, who was still standing politely in the doorway.

"Okay," said Foster, "come out with it. What are you selling? And don't try to tell me you're taking a survey or something. We had that one."

"Take me to your leader," said the Martian politely, just as he'd been taught in rocket school.

"I think he's got something to do with Atomic Appliances," said Mrs. Foster, coming to the door and wiping her hands on her apron. "They've always got some gimmick or other."

But Fred Foster had been feeling the Martian, pulling at its ears and fiddling with its antennas. "By george," he said. "I believe the fellow *is* a Martian!"

"Of course," said Mona. "I'd know him anywheres."

"Well for heaven's sake, invite the man in," said Mrs. Foster. "I'll just make some nice iced tea."

So they asked the Martian into the sitting room and they all sat down and looked at him while Mrs. Foster got the iced tea ready.

The Martian refused the iced tea politely and also the chocolate-chip cookies. But when the Persian cat jumped up on his lap, he ate that instead, fur and all. The Fosters were a bit put out, but didn't like to say anything since the Martian was company.

"Take me to your leader," the Martian said, looking around wistfully for another cat.

"By george, he's right," said Fred Foster. "This is one of those diplomatic things."

"Who *is* our leader?" Mona asked him.

Well now, there was a poser. Mrs. Foster insisted that it was the mayor, but Fred held out for the premier.

"Now, hold on, Fred," said Mrs. Foster. "If you're going to go to the top, then you have to go right to the secretary of state or maybe even to the prime minister."

"You've hit it, Mother!" said Fred Foster. "The prime minister, of course. This Martian comes from another country, don't he? Well, then he has to meet the head of a *country.* I'll just go and call up the prime minister now."

So he put in a long-distance call to Ottawa and made it person-to-person just in case the prime minister should be away on a trip or something. But he did not get him, only a young man whose name sounded like Grlb and who assured Fred Foster that he could speak for his chief.

"Well, all right," said Fred Foster. "Look, we've got a Martian here. He's landed in our back yard in one of those saucer things that they've been seeing around and he wants to go up to Ottawa and meet the prime minister personally."

The young man wasn't in the least surprised. He said that Mr. Foster would get a letter about it, and two days later the letter came:

> *The Prime Minister has asked me to tell you how very interested he was in your experience Saturday last and how much he appreciates your taking the trouble to call him personally regarding it.*
>
> *He has expressed the hope that should you ever be in Ottawa you will drop in to the visitors' gallery of*

the House of Commons and watch the democratic
process of this great nation in action.
>   *Sincerely yours,*
>   REGINALD GLRB
>   *Assistant to the Prime Minister*

This didn't seem very satisfactory.

"Maybe we ought to call the newspapers," said Mrs. Foster. The Martian was becoming a bit of a nuisance. He lived most of the time in his flying saucer, but periodically he would appear at the door and plaintively say, "Take me to your leader."

So Fred Foster got on the phone to a huge metropolitan daily, which I will not name here so that no one can say I am biased. The newspaperman who answered was very interested in the flying-saucer story. Fred could hear him scribbling furiously.

"Come out and see for yourself," said Fred Foster, but the reporter said that wouldn't be necessary; they could get all the details by phone and thus catch the home edition.

That afternoon there was a hilarious story on the second front page about Fred Foster's Martian, illustrated by comic cartoons. The story was immediately copied by the other two huge metropolitan papers, and the following day, sparing no expense, one of them actually sent a reporter to see the Fosters. The Fosters invited him into the sitting room, where he photographed all of them and took down some more quotes for his paper.

"The Martian's out back in his saucer," said Fred Foster. "Come on now and I'll show him to you."

But the reporter looked at his watch and said he really didn't have time, if he was going to catch the early edition and beat the other papers with his pix. He said he had all he needed, anyway; they probably wouldn't use more than two folios of copy, or maybe even just captions under a three-column photo on page three. Which was the way it turned out.

"MARTIAN" SLEPT HERE, according to Fred J. Forster (centre) of 224B Cecil St., Mrs. Forster (left), and daughter Mona, 14 (right), point to the spot on couch where they claim visitor from Mars sat and drank iced tea.

The following night the little Martian (who wasn't actually a Martian, but certainly an alien) took off in his flying saucer feeling a bit frustrated. He landed in a back yard in Poughkeepsie, New York, knocked on the door and started all over again: "Take me to your leader," he said hopefully.

He had been doing it for six and a half years without getting anywhere. He was a very stubborn Martian.

Two

LIFE IN THE OLDEN DAYS

Time present and time past
Are both perhaps present in time future,
And time future contained in time past.
T. S. Eliot

THE WAY WE WERE

WASHINGTON—*Top space experts said today that within 10 years men could be landing on Mars, reaching out for Jupiter, living in space stations and telecasting to all the world. One expert said that men within 40 years may be flashing to the stars and galaxies at the speed of light, 186,000 miles per second ....*
—From an old, old news story published in the late twentieth century

It is hard for us, in this modern age, to realize how our grandparents lived, back in the twentieth century. In many respects their life is to be envied, for it was a leisurely existence, free from those worries and cares that beset modern man, a golden period when the world moved slowly, an unhurried era where man had time to pause in the day's occupation and contemplate the beauty of the world around him.

The previous century, our grandparents, in their heavy and awkward clothing, were still driving crude hand-operated vehicles at speeds that—though this is difficult to believe—rarely exceeded eighty or ninety miles per hour. Indeed, some of the old "newspapers" tell us that on occasion, people were actually fined and even imprisoned for attaining this velocity!

Still, this is understandable when one realizes that as primitive as they were, the vehicles in those days were fantastically restricted in their movements. In the first place, they could not leave the ground. Second, they were required by law to stay on certain routes, so incredibly narrow that it was often impossible for more than two of them to drive abreast. These lanes were so badly constructed that they were constantly being repaired.

And yet, in spite of these obvious disadvantages, we cannot look back on the era now without a certain nostalgia. Everything was so simple in those far-off days. Our grandparents enjoyed simple pleasures: innocent dances and stories told on the "television" set, gay old tunes on the "record player," crudely photographed fables, many of them hand-coloured, projected in barn-like buildings called "theatres," to which the people of the time flocked by the hundreds.

Back in those days, people needed those simple pleasures. To a great extent they had to make their own fun; it was not manufactured for them as it is in our day. Travel, of course, was extremely limited and almost non-existent. Man was confined entirely to his own planet, and even then seldom ventured more than a few hundred miles from his abode. A family living in New York, for instance, might see their relatives in Los Angeles or in London, England, only once a year—and sometimes even less frequently!

Communication was even more difficult and awkward. Over short distances, people communicated by means of a curious device known as the "telephone." The method of use was rather complicated, but it was possible for a persevering and determined person to speak to a friend by means of this instrument. It was used, however, rather sparingly.

Living as he did in virtual isolation, chained to his own community by the strictures of the age, unable to communicate in any facile fashion except by the use of his own vocal cords, twentieth-century man had to find his strengths within the family structure. We may well envy the warm attachments of kinship that existed in those days. Men seldom married more than three or four times, and there are even cases where children remained with the same set of parents for all of their formative years.

The picture of family life in those days is charming and quaint, indeed, and some of its accoutrements have come down to us in the nostalgic songs of the age: the "recreation room" where games like "Ping-Pong" and "darts" were played; the "buffet supper" of fond memory; the "cocktail party," a social rite that some people living today can still recall; and, of course, the old-fashioned "barbecue pit," which children of today hear about at their grandmother's knee.

The young people, too, seemed to have been better behaved in those times. There was an air of courtliness and good breeding that has, alas, largely been lost. The teenaged youths in their black leather jackets, the young girls in their simple blue jeans, singing and dancing together with obvious joy; the slow and stately "rock-'n'-roll" tunes characteristic of those early days—well may we sigh for a return to these old values.

In spite of the incredibly long work day and unbelievable work week, in spite of the short span of life (a mere eighty or ninety years!), in spite of the total lack of modern labour-saving devices as we know them, the people of those times managed to move with an unhurried tread.

Breakfast was a leisurely affair, often occupying five or six minutes. The man of the house often lingered over his coffee before setting out for his place of work, which was seldom more than twenty or thirty miles distant!

Indeed, by our standards, the people of the last century had very little to worry about. Their life was as uncomplicated as their quaint vehicles. They worked hard and long, but they worked well. And they made do as best they could with what little leisure time they had, giving scant heed to the future, their minds uncluttered by any real knowledge of that solar system that was still as mysterious to them as heaven itself.

If someone had told them something of the world as we, their grandchildren and great-grandchildren, know it, they would have called him mad. And even had they believed a fraction of it to be true, it is probable that the people of the twentieth century would have chosen to remain in their own year, where life, gentle and untroubled, meandered like a languorous stream. Who, really, could blame them?

TWENTIETH-CENTURY ARTIFACTS

Professor Rodney Stanfield's recent archaeological expedition to the former site of Toronto, one of the ancient cities of the Old World, has been highly successful. Professor Stanfield's excavations, painstakingly carried out over a three-year period, have produced many new artifacts that cast further light on the lives of the primitive peoples who inhabited this area in the twentieth century. Reproductions of some of the chief finds are shown below:

This particularly fine example of twentieth-century art was one of several unearthed during Professor Stanfield's dig. However, this is the only one that he was able to maintain intact. The flask, obviously in common use at the time, preserves all the naïve art and primitive vigour of a people who love to work with their hands and—in spite of their many vicissitudes—enjoyed a zest for liquid refreshment.

Note the classic lines, simple and yet authoritative, of this roadside god, whose effigy appeared at regular intervals along thoroughfares of the day. Natives propitiated the deity with regular offerings of small metal pieces on which had been carved, with great ingenuity, the face of their leader or chieftain.

Cunningly wrought from preserved skins of domestic animals, this fetish was carried everywhere by the males of the tribe, who apparently believed that its possession conferred good fortune upon them. Without it, they felt lost, almost naked. Its presence gave a sense of power and confidence, and a feeling of "belonging."

Hand-carved clubs of various styles, many of them beautifully wrought, were chief weapons of the period. Tribes fought with them incessantly, and even children were drawn into warfare. The circular object (right) came equipped with string so it could be retrieved by its user after the enemy was bested.

Professor Stanfield and his researchers had great difficulty identifying this object, believing as they did that all cooking was done within the dwelling. As these and similar artifacts were always found in the back yard or native *patio*, he is forced to conclude that they were used for animal sacrifices to the various gods of the day. This theory is fortified by the discovery of heavily charred animal meat in the near vicinity.

These beautifully designed garments (*aprons*) are believed to have been worn by holy men presiding at sacrificial rites. Animal juices staining many samples reinforce this theory. Note the delicacy of the workmanship and the sophistication of the native drawings, which show high ability and a fundamental understanding of both art and taste. The natives were obviously highly developed in such skills and handicrafts.

MAMMOTH AIRLINES ANNUAL REPORT

M r. Chairman, members of the board of directors, and shareholders of Mammoth Airlines, Inc. It gives me great pleasure to present this, your company's fiftieth annual report in this, our silver anniversary year. Ours has truly been a story of progress in transportation and I think everyone in the great Mammoth family appreciates the strides we have made since the late twentieth century.

I can remember the early pioneering days when it actually took four or five hours to cross the continent by jet and even longer to traverse the ocean between America and Europe. Now, as you know, these things are accomplished in a matter of minutes.

Do you realize what this means, gentlemen? It means that a man can leave his home in a New York suburb at 6 a.m. and be absolutely sure of arriving at his hotel room in Paris within twenty-four hours—or at the very most thirty hours—of his departure. If it weren't for the scientific advances in aircraft design, allowing speeds of up to 3,000 mph, it would now take at least a day and a half or perhaps two days to cross the ocean by air, when you figure in limousine time, customs and immigration clearances, security checks, baggage problems, checking in, ticketing, and so on.

As you know, Mammoth Airlines absolutely insists that all its transatlantic passengers be at the airport checking-in counter four and one-half hours prior to their departure. Our new aircraft, I'm proud to say, are now equipped to hold 3,500 passengers if they are willing to travel by our new Peasant Class and engage in a bit of bundling. That's a lot of people to process through a few wickets.

Indeed, I have it in my mind to ask the board today to give me the necessary authority to detach seven of our aircraft designers from their normal duties in order that they might spend the next twelve months devising some new type of check-in counter with, say, three or four wickets. This could cut half an hour or even more off our present Waiting Room time.

I know that will involve a heavy expenditure since we will have to hire extra ticketing personnel, but our motivational people tell me that they do sense a certain amount of customer resistance regarding our present facilities. The unfortunate maiming of one of our flight attendants last week by a passenger who spent seven hours on the phone, vainly trying to reconfirm his overseas reservation, does suggest that some further modernization is necessary.

The handling of meals has presented more of a problem,

especially on transoceanic flights where, because of the time differential, we are committed to serving two seven-course meals to our Luxurious- and Super-Luxurious-Class passengers. This has proved a near superhuman task for the complement of seven flight attendants, especially since these classes normally serve seven hundred people and the actual in-flight time is only twenty-six minutes. Remember also that the cabin has to be pitch dark so that everybody can watch the movie.

We are now developing an ingenious system to meet these difficulties and allow us to maintain our own lucrative luxury trade. Luxurious-Class passengers will now be served two courses—hors d'oeuvres and soup—while waiting in line at the check-in counter (and, I may add, in full view of envious Peasant-Class passengers). On boarding the aircraft they will pick up a tray—as in a cafeteria—and select two more courses from an automatic machine. The final three courses will be served to them in the terminal at their destination while they wait for their baggage, a period that normally occupies one or two hours owing to the large number of people now being accommodated by our new jet transports.

This still leaves a second seven-course meal, and I must say our solution, worked out by a team of efficiency experts, is a real winner. The second meal will be served in the limousine. Thus, gentlemen, we solve two problems neatly: First, we maintain the high standards of service that make our Luxurious-Class a continuing status symbol, and second, we do much to alleviate those unfortunate spells of faintness, dizziness, and malnutrition that some passengers were suffering as a result of long hours spent confined in various forms of ground transportation.

Our Peasant-Class standards, of course, will also be maintained, as always, at mere subsistence level in order to increase the desirability of the higher-priced tickets.

Actually, we are hoping that the new Toronto International Preston Manning Airport, when it is completed, will solve many of these problems. Our subsidiary company, Airport Limousines, Inc., is particularly pleased with the new location at Orillia, since this will allow them to institute a long overdue increase in fares.

I am hopeful that the extra time involved in reaching the new terminal will be at least partially absorbed by more efficient ticketing procedures. But, of course, Mammoth Airlines cannot be responsible for traffic conditions between Toronto and Orillia.

Meanwhile, I am happy to announce another price reduction in domestic fares—a long-standing policy commitment by your company, which believes in passing on to the customer those savings made possible by scientific progress. Henceforth for Peasant-Class passengers, the fare to Vancouver from Toronto will be a mere $5,425.70. This means that, when limousine, parking, and airport-hotel space are considered, a man can fly one way to Vancouver for as little as $6,237.50. A real step forward if I may say so.

As you know, your company was one of the very first to show full-length late-release, wide-screen motion pictures on our Luxurious-Class flights, both transcontinental and transoceanic. This far-sighted policy increased our competitive position within the industry and helped give us an enviable 17.08 percent increase in Luxurious-Class fares during the first decade of operation.

We have ironed out most of the problems that these movies caused when the new jet service was instituted last year. As you know, the actual flight time between Toronto and Vancouver is now only seventeen minutes, and many passengers protested that they were missing most of the film.

To resolve this understandable difficulty, your company has instituted a policy whereby Luxurious-Class passengers arrive at the airport an hour earlier than Peasant-Class and Superpeasant-Class. Here they are shown the start of the film. On arrival at their destination they are ushered directly into a special theatre and shown the remainder of the film. This has proved extremely popular since we have discovered that most Luxurious-Class passengers aren't in that much of a hurry anyway.

WHEN CIGARETTES WERE BANNED

When cigarettes were finally banned for medical reasons in every civilized country, promoters the world over began to search around for something that could safely take their place. Bubblegum was mentioned briefly, but it was agreed that (except in the case of six-year-olds) it did not give you that "lift," so important in any popular habit-forming preparation. Salted peanuts, which are *almost* as habit-forming, enjoyed a mild boom, but this was short-lived. The sales of certain cola drinks also shot up for a time, but even though they made people young and fair and debonair, they also made them fat, and so never achieved the popularity of tobacco.

What was wanted, obviously, was something habit-forming and cheap that gave you an immediate lift, kept you slim, never got on your nerves, was mild and relaxing—that, in a pinch, you would Walk a Mile For.

At one point, gin was suggested as the perfect substitute, but it turned out that everybody was drinking all the gin they could get, anyway. The market was saturated, like the customers.

Could nothing replace cigarettes? The best minds in advertising had grappled with the problem in vain. And yet, somewhere, everybody knew there must be some preparation that could be put into easy, everyday use and make a billion for its developer.

The man who finally came up with it was none other than Rogers Tyrrel, who had been the greatest tobacco tycoon of all time. Since Prohibition, Tyrrel had scarcely been heard from. Even his closest enemies (he had no friends) had no idea what he was up to. Then, when it was too late and he had cornered the market, it slowly dawned on them. Tyrrel had been operating a vast, subtle lobby at all world capitals with one single purpose in mind: to make dope legal.

Tyrrel had instantly realized that only one thing could replace tobacco: opium and its derivatives, morphine and heroin. And why not? Tyrrel reasoned. Nobody could say dope didn't give you a big lift; nobody could say it didn't relax your nerves, pep you up, make you forget your cares; and what's more, *nobody could say it caused lung cancer.*

This was the point that Tyrrel's subtle lobbyists hammered at hardest: dope didn't cause cancer. It didn't cause heart disease either. As long as you kept taking it, it didn't cause much of anything. Why not legalize it, then, and end the vicious dope racket that kept the police forces of the globe occupied? Most burglaries, much prostitution, half the world's vice was the result of making dope illegal. Make it easy to get, Tyrrel whispered, and you'd lick the crime problem, save the taxpayers money, and keep the voters happy.

When the politicians finally gave in, Tyrrel was ready with a huge advertising campaign and plenty of merchandise. Twenty-four-sheet billboards appeared on all the highways showing a sumptuously gowned woman bringing a grateful husband his slippers and needle. The caption read: FIVE O'CLOCK, DARLING! TIME FOR YOUR FIX. Millions of matchbooks were printed for distribution in bars. They bore the simple slogan: GET ON THE STUFF! A singing commercial played on every radio station in the land became so popular that the kiddies were even singing its theme: DON'T BE A DOPE! USE DOPE!

Meanwhile, the shelves of every drugstore, cigar store, and supermarket were piled high with Tyrrel's neat little kits containing small packets of capsules, tourniquets, small bent spoons, and chromium-plated needles. The needles came in three sizes: Light, Medium, and Heavy (for those who liked the heft and feel of a heavy needle).

It was Tyrrel's purpose to get everybody hooked properly as soon as possible, and he swiftly convinced most of the world that it was un-American to be anything but a habitual user.

In the slick women's magazines four-colour ads hammered the message home. Pretty girls were shown, needle in hand, with handsome, virile men, over a caption that read: MY BILL'S A REAL GUY! HE'S RIGHT ON THE MAIN LINE!

Tyrrel in his dope campaign had concentrated pretty well on selling the stuff to men. But rivals were soon in the field with dope of their own, and the fight was on to get the women to take it. For some time it had been considered rather coarse for a woman to use a needle in public. Several ad campaigns now concentrated on removing this stigma.

REACH FOR A NEEDLE INSTEAD OF A SWEET was one very effective slogan of the day. The makers of Sherlock's (a brand of white heroin that showed the famous detective, needle in hand, on the box) had a similar campaign: IT'S THE REAL THING! their ads read. Pictures showed happy, laughing young people, faultlessly dressed in expensive evening clothes, standing around a home barbecue and jabbing needles into their arms the New, Modern Way.

The Madison Avenue boys, back on the job again, drove home the idea that it was fashionable to take dope. TV stars, baseball heroes, playboys, and society girls appeared in ads and on the home screen making such impromptu statements as: "Man, oh, man, when it comes to deep down, satisfying relaxation, there's nothing like a big, refreshing deck of Super-Tyrrel Morphine!" Or: "After twelve hours under the studio lights, I can hardly wait to get back on the Stuff again." Or: "Ladies, ask yourself this question: is your husband irritable, nervous, out of sorts lately? Maybe he's trying to kick the habit. Take lovely Marcia Keene's advice: ease his nerves tonight with a full needle of Yak's Opium. Remember, Yak's never gets on your nerves!"

The dope industry faced only one crisis, and that was short-lived. Certain research scientists claimed to have discovered that the persistent jabs on the upper arms were causing cancer of the skin. The industry met the charges head on. First, it produced scientists of its own to show that the medical evidence was tenuous and incomplete. But, more important, it began producing new filter needles, which were Milder to Your Skin and Removed Harmful Irritants. After a brief slump, dope sales soared to new records. People simply switched to the new needles and stopped worrying about harmful effects. As Rogers Tyrrel remarked (puffing away at an illegal cigarette), what else could you expect of a bunch of dopes?

NEW FADS IN THE FUNERAL INDUSTRY

Mr. Chairman, honoured guests, ladies and gentlemen. It is a considerable honour and, I may add, a distinct pleasure for me to address this giant convention on the subject of progress in the funeral industry. Many of you may ask why I have chosen this particular subject for my centenary address. Today funeral practices seem to us to have reached an acme of perfection. But old-time funerologists will know whereof I speak.

The fact is, ladies and gentlemen, that it was not until the twentieth century that the modern funeral industry can be said to have had its beginnings. It is hard to realize now what a crude thing a funeral was back then. Some people paid less than $2,000 for the entire business! Caskets were plain and unadorned. Embalming was in its infancy—so elementary, indeed, that after two or three days on display, the dead were hidden away from view in a shallow pit known as a "grave," marked by some inconspicuous monument.

The modern term "funerologist" had not then been put into common use. Funerologists were called "morticians" or "funeral directors," terms that came in for a certain amount of opprobrium. In addition to the stigma of the name, many in the industry felt that the old designations failed to adequately describe the host of duties and services that a modern funerologist performs. Hence, a title with more dignity and meaning was devised.

It was public demand, of course, that forced the funeral industry to modernize, and the complaint of some churchmen that the profit motive was the sole impetus for the Big Change is groundless. The public simply demanded a higher quality of service, and since service is our motto, we were obliged to give it to them.

The first big change, I suggest, came with the switch from the casket to the modern Funeral Couch. For some years the public had been demanding coloured caskets, and whites, creams, beiges, and rich browns, but with the introduction of the Princess Casket in Sea Foam Green, Lapis Lazuli Blue, Peach Glow, Egyptian Saffron, and Boudoir Pink, the change was complete. Later, the public insisted on a more fashionable colour, Scandal Scarlet, to match the new cars and lipsticks, and, of course, we gave it to them. I am proud to say that we now have Funeral Couches in 727 beautiful shades, ranging from Fire Chief Orange to Bourbon Beige.

One of the real problems the old-time mortician faced was the attempt to convince the bereaved that their Loved One was not actually dead but only slumbering. This difficulty was heightened by the presence of a hinged lid on the casket. When that lid shut it was awfully hard to convince the common man that death wasn't real! (LAUGHTER)

The Funeral Couch, with its Plexiglas top, changed all that. The public loved it, and, of course, the funerologists were pleased because it showed their handiwork to a far, far better effect. A real stroke of genius came with the introduction of a tiny record player within the Couch itself that reproduced, with perfect fidelity, the heavy breathing of the deceased. This was the main feature of our major model change and it increased Couch sales in that one year alone by 27.3 percent—a real triumph for the industry and a milepost in our pioneering history. (APPLAUSE)

Of course, some of you young people have forgotten or maybe didn't ever know that the conception of the yearly models is less than a century old in our particular business. The public demanded it, of course, after the introduction of the prefabricated Family Vault. Up until that time our ancestors had been digging holes in the ground to stash their Loved Ones in, but the concept of the Vault in Every Home changed all that. The public was very receptive to that idea, which is the basis and foundation of the modern funeral industry, an industry which, I may proudly add, has grown to that of second place in this burgeoning nation, right after pulp and paper.

For some time, of course, there had been consumer resistance to the idea of purchasing an expensive casket and then covering it with earth so that the neighbours couldn't see it. The wealthier classes had already seen the advantages of displaying their investment in large family vaults, but the mass-produced prefabricated Vault for basement, garage, or rumpus room brought the concept to millions. When television palled, it became the socially accepted practice to invite friends down to the Vault to view one's ancestors breathing realistically beneath their Plexiglas covers. Far better than leafing through a musty old family album, as the funerologists of the day were quick to point out!

In the subsequent half of the century we have seen much more emphasis placed on the Funeral Couch. As the years rolled by, the public demanded better-designed Couches and, of course, the industry, with its concept of service, stepped into the breach. Soon it ceased to be socially acceptable to have an outmoded Funeral Couch —or outmoded accessories, for that matter—in one's Vault. Some of you older fellows will probably remember the year that coloured shrouds came in and the big run there was on those. Yes, accessories have become a vital part of our business, as those of you who attended the Clothing Seminar and heard that inspiring panel discussion on Footwear for the Sleeping will attest to. The old phrase "I wouldn't be seen dead in that suit!" has taken on a new meaning, I can tell you! (LAUGHTER)

Although the yearly model change and planned obsolescence in Funeral Couches seemed to place the accent on accoutrements, I do not mean to suggest that we have ever, for one single moment, neglected the Loved Ones who are, after all, our *raison d'être*—if I may be allowed to slip, briefly, into a foreign tongue. No, no; far from it! A healthy and thriving industry has recently sprung up with the single purpose of supplying food and other essentials for the Loved Ones. These packaged goods, together with pets, books, games, small portable television sets, and (for the women) fresh cosmetics, are made specially for the new-model Funeral Couches. The idea is that if the Slumberer should ever Awaken, all his needs will be instantly provided for. It has been a great comfort to the public, which has long demanded such a change, and, I might add, a mighty profitable sideline for some of our confrères.

As for many of our customers, friends—well, I can only wind up this brief address with our long-standing motto: None of them ever kicked yet! (LAUGHTER AND PROLONGED APPLAUSE)

WHERE'LL WE GO ON OUR HOLIDAYS?

George, what do you say we take our holidays in the winter for once? I mean, with the summer so nice and all, it's a shame, really, to go away.

Well, that suits me okay, Gert. Where was you thinking of going?

Oh, anywhere, I don't mind, so long's we get away from the rat race.

Well then, how about the Moon? I hear they got things fixed up pretty good there, now.

The Moon! Oh, George, really! *Everybody* goes to the Moon. Use a little imagination, for gosh sakes.

Well, I dunno. I was talking to old Fred Wagsby just the other day and he says he and Netty had a really wonderful time on the Moon. He says now that the new Moon-Hilton is operating, it's just like a home away from home.

I'd expect that from Fred Wagsby. They never go anywhere except to the tourist traps. Honestly, George, the people in the know will tell you the Moon's real junky. It's too resorty. Just a bunch of cheap, noisy nightclubs and tourist hotels. And the prices! I hear they've gone sky high.

Gee, Gert, I'd always understood you could pick up a lot of that native stuff for a song.

Not like ten years ago! The tourists have ruined it for everybody. That's what everybody says. They've driven up the price out of all reason. Everything's phony up there now, believe me, George. Alice Grayson was saying just the other morning how a few years back you could sample some really authentic Moon dishes and watch colourful Moon dancers down by the craters and all that, but not anymore. It's all become terribly commercialized.

I'd sort of set my heart on taking one of those crater tours. Always did want to see a Moon crater.

You'd be terribly disappointed, George, honest you would. They've got neon signs and hot-dog stands all over the craters now and the guides really rook you. Alice Grayson says so. They really see you coming.

Well, I guess that sort of lets the Moon out.

George! What do you say we just pack a couple of bags and steal off to Venus? It's absolutely unspoiled on the far side, according to *Holiday* magazine, and you can live there for next to nothing. Jack and Rita Frabnash were there last week and they had this big place with Venusian servants for only half a million a week! Think of it, George!

I'm thinking of it and I don't like it. In the first place, the rocket service is lousy. You got to change at Mars and there's always a dreadful wait on the satellite. If there's one thing I don't want to do, it's spend half my vacation in satellite lounges waiting for my flight to be called.

But, George—think of when we get there! Rita Frabnash says this place of theirs was completely off the beaten track. You'd never believe you were only a few million miles from home. Honestly, she says it was fabulous. They could see the thorks come down to the watering hole from their window at night.

Not for me. I'm fed up with that lousy native food. It's okay the first day, but I don't want it as a steady diet. Say what you want about the Moon, but at least you can get real Earth cooking and room service when you want it. Personally, I'd a lot sooner go off to Jupiter and get in some Jasper hunting. Some of the other boys was talking about making up a party.

Well, if you think that's any holiday for me, you're very much mistaken. Sitting around the lodge twiddling my thumbs all day while you and that pack of ruffians go off after Jaspers and spend half your time getting tanked up on Jupiter Juice! No, thanks!

Well, it was only a suggestion. Gert, look, I got an idea. How about taking one of those luxury package tours around the solar system? The new spaceships got everything, you know, sundeck, swimming pools, shuffleboard—really fabulous. There's dancing every night to three orchestras and a special side tour, optional, to see the rings of Saturn. Sounds great, eh, baby?

I don't know, George. Ellie Rathbog went two seasons back and she said it was really rough every day but one. She couldn't keep anything solid in her stomach, so the whole thing was a washout as far as she was concerned.

Well, now look, Gert, I got something in mind and I think I might just swing it financially. Whaddaya say we buy ourselves a small asteroid and put a cottage on it? Nothing fancy—just a place we could go up to on weekends, put our feet up on the porch rail, and look at the sunset.

An asteroid! George, are you out of your mind?

What's wrong with an asteroid, Gert?

Well, in the first place all the good ones have been taken long ago. In the second place, you never know who your neighbours are. Everybody says that the Martians have practically taken them over. Loud, vulgar people!

Oh, come on now, Gert, we know quite a few Martians. They ain't so bad.

Mind you, George, I've got nothing personal against Martians. I never said that. I've known a lot of very fine Martians and some of my dearest friends are Martians, for that matter. I don't mind them singly; it's just that when you get them in a crowd that they get pushy.

We'd have the asteroid to ourselves, Gert. Just you and me and the kids.

Yes, but how would you like it if the asteroids next door were all owned by Martians and their kids were climbing onto our asteroid all the time. Say what you like, George, but when you get away on a holiday you want to be surrounded by your own kind.

Where are we going to go on our vacation, Gert?

Whaddaya say we just stay home for once, George?

You mean just hang around Earth?

Sure, go downtown to Miami some night, or Paris, maybe. Fool around Rome and Calcutta in the mornings.

You'd be surprised how many people are doing just that, George.

Okay by me, Gert. At least we'll save ourselves a few million bucks that way.

REMEMBER WHEN CHRISTMAS WAS FOR REAL?

The campaign to decommercialize Christmas began slowly and modestly, but after a few years it gathered surprising momentum.

It began in one of the universities as a kind of joke, but before the semester was out a good many students were taking it seriously. Within a year they formed the Combined Universities Campaign for a Decommercialized Christmas, with chapters on every campus.

At first the kids were considered more a nuisance than anything—carrying placards in the Santa Claus parade (demanding it be abolished), staging sit-downs in Toyland, picketing stationery shops to urge a ban on Christmas cards, and going on hunger strikes on the day itself. But then came the daring night raid on the Noma Lite factory. The resultant court case brought the campaign instant world recognition. This was the spark that touched off the famous People's Movement Against the Man Who Has Everything, an adult organization dedicated to ridiculing and denouncing foolish Christmas giving.

The PMAMWHE (as it was universally called) began to publish a Blacklist of Foolish Christmas Presents, which caused a widespread public reaction. A torn fragment of a catalogue is still available and may have some historical interest. It is a genuine list of nationally advertised Christmas gifts, circa 1961, and it includes:

- The Target Beer-Can Launcher ("Fire your empty beer cans forty feet in the air for safe, easy target practice")
- The Effortless Electric Carving-Knife Set ("Battery-operated electric knife will give professional touch to your carving")
- The Life-Size Santa Doorman ("It identifies YOUR home with YOUR family name!")
- The Fun-Lovin' Warm-Up Jacket ("Boldly lettered with funny, imaginary names like USA Drinking Team")
- The Glamour Girl Ice-Cube Maker ("Put more fun in your drinks with these unusual ice cube cuties")
- The Adorable Personalized Reindeer ("With YOUR child's name, hand decorated, for a lovable Christmas decoration"), and
- The Five O'Clock Cocktail Watch ("Never drink before five? Rejoice, your worries are over, because it's always five o'clock with this watch").

The publication of this list, with the resultant wave of universal revulsion, drove several huge manufacturing firms right out of business. PMAMWHE's sponsors shrewdly played up the idea that only simple, home-made Christmas gifts gave you real Status. Pretty soon people got Top Status by not giving any gifts at all.

One man who distributed a patented Moon Scale to all his friends ("Gives both Moon weight and Earth weight at the same time; just the ticket for the man who has everything") was subjected to such ridicule that he committed suicide, using a Mr. and Mrs. King-Size Giant Punch Combination Can and Bottle Opener (described by its makers as a "fantastic conversation piece").

Then there was the famous incident of the inflatable lawn Santa Claus in Goosequill, Manitoba. This was a gargantuan effigy, floodlit in four colours, which a J. Robinson Squill had insisted on erecting despite his neighbours' protests. Mr. Squill had purchased the Santa Claus in the days when it was an okay thing to have one on his lawn. Indeed, he had been forced into it by his children under social pressure and, as he was still paying instalments on it, he felt he ought to get his money's worth. A howling mob stoned his home and the Squills had to call the police for protection. The Santa Claus was destroyed, and the incident effectively marked the end of Christmas accessories.

This led to a significant act of Parliament banning the playing of Christmas carols on any radio or TV station or in any public place except a church. That really ended Christmas music. When a popular singer named Goon Wiseman (a member of a singing group called the Three Wisemen) tried to record a rock version of "Adeste Fideles," the Legion of Decency boycotted all his work. That ended the Christmas record business.

Soon Christmas was just another day. The police didn't even have to give traffic warnings, and so the number of deaths and accidents rose again to a refreshingly normal figure. The day remained a holiday in most cities, but since the idea of bloating oneself on turkey to the point of illness had become socially taboo, there wasn't much to do except watch the fights on television or, of course, go to church.

The reaction to all this can be traced to a best-selling book titled *Remember When Christmas Was for Real?* This remarkable volume evoked with something akin to poetry all the nostalgia of the old-fashioned Christmas of the twentieth century. It told of the crowded streets, jammed with Santa Clauses of every size and description ... the wonderful trees of pink and gold plastic ... of department stores that were fairylands of glittering lights and collapsing shoppers ... of motorists full of the daring that only a Yuletide *joie de vivre* can bring ... of tiny children paying out their buck and a half to be photographed with Santa ... of liquor stores jammed almost as full as food banks ... and of the air filled with music—even at 4 a.m.

The effect of this book (which was serialized, expanded, condensed, abridged, rewritten, stolen, paraphrased, imitated, and adapted as a hit song) was to conjure up a vision that, in those bleak days, was altogether charming. For it told how, in that wonderful bygone era, every day was a Christmas Day. Youngsters were astonished to learn that Christmas began before Halloween and that, as Valentine's Day approached, people were still exchanging presents (at the exchange counters).

The book was so successful that, when a discount house in Garbagevale, Saskatchewan, hesitantly installed a Santa Claus on its main floor, it stopped traffic.

That did it. The following year Air Canada's *enRoute* magazine, in its Christmas issue, featured a Useless Gift from the Past. It was a replica of the Do-It-Yourself Transistorized Pocket Lie Detector, which had been advertised away back in 1991. The device proved an instant hit.

Slowly, like a rusty machine, the great Christmas industry began to move into high gear. A man named Skeeters Ratchet recorded "Joy to the World" in scat talk and sold a million platters. An inventor in Snarl, Virginia, devised a combination Christmas tree and coat-rack that was a fabulous success. And in Goosequill, one J. Robinson Squill, now an old man, bought himself a grotesque inflatable Santa Claus suitable for lawn display to the applause of almost everybody.

THE DAY THE POPULATION EXPLODED

It was not until the twenty-first century that the sub-divisions began to cause real trouble. Until that time they had been merely a nuisance, spreading out from the ever-expanding cities in concentric circles, the lots growing tinier by the decade.

The first of the farmers' riots occurred in mid-century on the outskirts of Winnipeg, a few miles from Regina. The immediate cause was a new subdivision, five hundred miles long, straddling the Trans-Canada Highway, and containing more than a quarter of a million identical machine-made homes, all on twenty-foot lots. It was hailed by the mayor of Winnipeg as "a milestone in progress." But it raised the assessment value of the neighbouring farmland so much that the crushing burden of taxes made agriculture impossible.

The revolt was quickly quelled by the RCMP, but it touched off further disturbances all over North America. A subdivider who had bulldozed a forest area near the

city limits of Calgary (not far from Edmonton) nar-
rowly escaped lynching. At San Diego, a suburb of Los
Angeles, a group of malcontents led a spirited attack on
bulldozers and destroyed three with Molotov cocktails.
The attack, alas, came too late to save the topsoil, which
had already been pushed into the Pacific Ocean.

But when the mayor of Metropolitan Toronto proudly
announced that the city had reached a population of 20
million, there were few complaints. This huge consumer
market, the mayor said, ensured the prosperity of the
city, which had outstripped the rosiest predictions of the
demographers. A few people muttered about the price
of bread, which had risen to five dollars a loaf because
of the wheat scarcity, and there was some nostalgia, too,
about the good old days of green vegetables. But it was
generally agreed that the draining of the Holland Marsh
and its conversion into a popular midtown apartment
district had been a magnificent engineering feat. As
the mayor said in his statement: "You just can't stop
progress."

Then, two curiously isolated incidents occurred, which,
in retrospect, take on considerable significance.

In Montreal, a green salad went on display in a
department-store window. The oddity attracted such
crowds that police had to be called in to get traffic moving.

In Los Angeles, in the congested Beverly Hills slum
district, a woman appeared in the street with six children, all her own. She was hissed at and spat upon by
neighbours.

Shortly after that, the first of the twenty-two-lane
highways was completed between Ottawa and Windsor.

It was designed for a speed of two hundred kph, but the traffic was so heavy on all the twenty-two lanes that a limit of twenty-five kph had to be set.

In 2055, the Manhattan BMI subway was completed to Philadelphia, whose limits began at the first subway exit. A special detail was appointed to control the heavy pedestrian traffic, which moved in designated lanes along the former New Jersey turnpike, now converted into a giant shopping centre.

A year later, Wal-Mart announced the construction of the world's largest supermarket, an edifice designed to occupy, under a single roof, the space once occupied by the former Borough of Brooklyn. The supermarket took in a former building that had occupied the entire space once occupied by Ebbet's Field.

By 2060, access to Central Park in New York City was rationed. Special tickets were provided monthly and each citizen was allowed thirty minutes to stroll in the greenery. Queues several miles long formed before the gates for the privilege. The gates were guarded by machine-guns.

Then in 2061, the Province of Ontario, following the lead of several U.S. states, banned all house building within its boundaries. A subdividers' lobby fought the legislation, but it was upheld by the Supreme Court. Special police details were appointed to ferret out house bootleggers attempting to construct log cabins at astronomical prices in the Precambrian bush country.

In 2063, in an unprecedented announcement from Buckingham Palace, England's young king stated that he would limit his family to a single heir, and called upon all patriotic Britons to follow suit. The popular press stepped up a campaign of vilification against people with large families.

By 2057, most countries had made it illegal to have more than three children. Three years later it became illegal to have more than two children. In 2075, there were only three countries left—Paraguay, Ghana, and Liechtenstein—where it was legal for a family to have more than a single child.

By 2080, every country in the world, except Madagascar, had outlawed the building of single-family detached homes and had made the occupation of any existing detached dwelling by a single family a serious crime. In Scottsbluff, Nebraska, that year, one Horace J. Simpkins was sentenced to seven years' imprisonment because he, his wife, two children, mother-in-law, and maiden aunt had occupied a four-room bungalow by themselves—this group being designated by the courts as "a family unit." The children were given three years' definite and two years' indefinite in the state reformatory. The judge, in his summing up, castigated the Simpkinses for having two children.

In 2085, the United States and Canada enacted federal laws making the unlicensed birth of any child a crime. Progressive elements hailed this as a "far-reaching piece of social legislation."

In 2090, in Chicago, the first mile-high apartment was completed to house 2,500 family units. Two hundred similar structures were in the construction stage. The same year, multiple-dwelling life became compulsory in ten states and three Canadian cities.

In 2100, when the U.S. population had reached a total of 915 billions, the federal government made all births illegal and suspended permits. Canada, as always, followed three years later. Legislation was enacted providing for the extermination of all children born illegally, and special "extermination depots" were set up across the country to administer the matter efficiently. A special detachment of the FBI was formed to delve into the backgrounds of all females to determine the number of illegal children. (This material was shared with the RCMP.) In the first six months, the U.S. Bureau of Statistics reported that 1,216,000 children between the ages of one week and twelve years had been exterminated. The Canadian figure was 417,000.

The report was considered most encouraging, since this figure represented a healthy 4.3 percent of the number of people who had died during the same period of starvation or trampling.

"We are," said the president, "well on the road to coming to grips with the population explosion."

Three

THE HARD SELL

If there were dreams to sell,
What would you buy?
Thomas Lovell Beddoes

WHAT ALGERNON STRINGER DID FOR COMMERCIALS

Is there a greater advertising genius extant than Algernon Stringer, president of the great ad agency of Slant, Burble, Krisp, Fodder, and Skreem? (known throughout the trade as SBKF and S?). I do not believe so, for Stringer is the acknowledged giant of the industry. Who remembers Slant, Burble, and Krisp? They have long since gone to their coronary rest, while Fodder and Skreem are mere names on a letterhead. But the slightest hint that Stringer is working on an account will send the sales graph to new Everests.

Since the very beginning Stringer has been dedicated to a single proposition: Time is something to be filled with commercial messages. Air that contains anything *other* than commercials is, to him, "dead air." I still remember him in his youth, fidgeting during the organ interlude at the Conrad Black Memorial Church, and trying to figure out a way to work in the tunes of two singing commercials between stanzas of "Shall We Gather at the River?" He was not successful, but he accomplished his aim in a roundabout way by commissioning a singing commercial for a finance company to the same melody. Thus, whenever any organist played that grand old hymn, the congregation was subtly reminded that they would be treated with dignity whenever they needed easy cash.

It used to bother Stringer to have to listen to CDs of great classical music because they were uninterrupted by any sponsored message. I have watched him literally writhe over the hi-fi set as the strains of Prokofiev poured out without a single commercial break. He felt, somehow, that the advertising world was being cheated by these "sustaining discs," as he called them.

His break came when he persuaded a small company, recording under the Shatter label, to sell commercial time on its jumbo release of Handel's *Messiah*. There were seven commercial spots in all, of forty-five seconds each, promoting Glib, the new fluoride toothpaste with the semisweet chocolate flavour. The alternate sponsor (on the flip side) was Jerm, the antiseptic mouthwash that tasted like vodka.

The disc was an instant hit, not only because it sold for slightly less money, being sponsored, but also because people genuinely enjoyed the commercial breaks: they were used to them from radio and TV. For some time, indeed, there had been a rising tide of indignation against the record companies for insisting on an uninterrupted flow of music. Stringer filled a genuine need—after all, that is the basis of good advertising—and the whole industry quickly fell in line.

An ingenious Stringer refinement was his master stroke in persuading famous concert recording artists to voice the commercials personally. Thus, Jascha Heifetz, just before the famous Joachim cadenza in the Beethoven Violin Concerto, set aside his bow for a moment to speak a few words in favour of Gurgle, the sensational new cola drink that maintains its fizz even when the cap is lost. All in good taste, of course. Small wonder that Stringer was given the Enterprise in Action Award at the annual convention of the Society for Prevention of Traditional Freedoms.

For Stringer this was only a beginning. His next coup was a major one. Single-handedly, he succeeded in selling commercial time on the pilots' announcements on Pan American Airways domestic and international flights. The original tape of Capt. Gerald Farber's remarks now rests in a glass case at the Creative Advertising Institute Museum. "Ladies and gentlemen, we will be flying at an altitude of 28,000 feet," it begins—and then the historic words follow: "And speaking of feet, folks, have you enjoyed an Acme Home Pedicure lately?"

These messages were an instant success and every airline quickly found it had to adopt the idea. Everyone agreed that they worked to soothe the hesitant air traveller—to make him feel as if he were right in the safety of his own living room.

Stringer's greatest stroke of genius had its genesis when he phoned a local radio station and heard the operator say: "Good morning. Radio station CHOO! Most-listened to station in your area by actual survey. May I help you?" Suddenly, it came to Stringer that commercial time could also be sold on telephone calls. A pilot project was instantly set up in twenty-six selected factories, business offices, and public institutions, and was enormously successful. The first test call is also on tape at the museum:

SWITCHBOARD: Simpkins Tool & Die. Good morning! And it *will* be a good morning if you start the day right with Vita-Whip, nature's own energizing cream.

CALLER: Give me Mr. Simpkins, please.

SWITCHBOARD: I will connect you with his secretary. But if you *really* want to make connections, don't forget that new all-purpose Groom strengthens hair follicles while giving your scalp new lustre.

SECRETARY: Mr. Simpkins' office. Can I help you— by recommending Whiff, the safe, all-purpose decongestant tablet?

CALLER: Give me J.A. It's rush.

SECRETARY: I'm sorry, Mr. Simpkins is not available. But Glare, the amazing hand lotion that shines like varnish, is *always* available at leading drugstores ...

Although one or two callers complained about delays, especially those phoning hospital emergency wards, most people quickly became used to phone commercials.

Stringer then moved quickly to sell commercials on long-distance calls. As he pointed out to the telephone companies, they had the perfect captive audience and there could be no argument about the ratings. It soon became commonplace for anybody placing a long-distance call to receive two commercial messages before being connected with his party.

Stringer's latest move is to have the commercial time increased by thirty seconds on person-to-person calls, but so far the CRTC has not approved the request. Advertising has its place, they agree, but they don't think it should take precedence over public service. In a democracy this is, of course, an arguable point. A good many people now think that the bureaucrats are again trying to deny us our basic freedoms.

THE TERRIBLE TOOTHPASTE CRISIS

LONDON *(Reuters)—Britons may soon be able to clean their teeth by popping a pill in their mouths. A British firm announced today the company had perfected a tablet that cleans teeth by stimulating the flow of saliva in the mouth.*

—Toronto Star, November 22, 1961

EASY DOES IT with Win Packer: Mrs. J. A. has asked us how she can remove a cloudy heat mark from her dining-room table. Put a dab of toothpaste on the mark and let stand for a few minutes, then rub with a soft cloth. A second application may be necessary ... More about versatile toothpaste (as a household cleaner) on another day.

—Toronto Star, December 6, 1961

The day that came to be known as Black Friday in the toothpaste business opened quite normally in the lush boardroom of the mammoth advertising firm of Lush, Glib, Rightworthy, Brash, and Footling. The room itself was a tribute to the quiet taste that distinguishes the industry. The cigar-shaped conference table of teak and sandalwood rested on a jet-black pile carpet of imported yak's hair, and this pleasing effect was nicely contrasted by pure-white walls of cushioned leather, studded with solid brass knurls.

Apart from the standard Alexander Calder mobile, the room was almost bare of decoration. An El Greco or two, a harlequin-period Picasso, and a small but exquisite Roualt were all that intruded upon the starkness of three walls. The fourth, however, was dominated by a poster on which an enormous smile had been reproduced eighteen times larger than life. The smile was dazzling in its brilliance—the teeth so perfectly fashioned that they seemed to have been carved out of Mount Rushmore. Underneath the smile a message proclaimed the eternal truth that SQUIRM IS A FUN TOOTH-PASTE.

The men assembled here on this fateful Friday morning were among the giants of the toothpaste business. It was they who had collectively and after careful motivational work designed the famous Tube with the Wiggle. Exhaustive surveys by Wedgwood J. Doggerel ("the Greatest Name in Testing") had established beyond doubt that the actual squeezing of the new Squirm tube released suppressed infantile sexual desires in 80.7 percent of all males tested and 68.1 percent of all women. Further, the observational work of Dr. Rheinhold von Griezbenzl proved conclusively that when toothpaste emerges from a tube in a zigzag fashion, people will normally use 1.83 times as much as when it emerges in a simple ribbon.

The Strategy Board of Squirm had a good reason to be satisfied with their product. It dominated the field. Now that the American Psychological Congress had actually given it guarded approval, it looked like nothing could stop it. Still, a good ad man never rests. For the past six months the creative branch of the agency had been working on an Amazing New Scientific Ingredient with which to strengthen Squirm (since Squirm was largely soap). Now it looked like young Forthright had something.

"Gentlemen," Basil J. Forthright was saying, "in this small jar we have distilled one of the greatest scientific discoveries known to man—a method of polishing the teeth to a whiteness hitherto unknown in the dentifrice field. Let me give you a demonstration."

He pointed to a cloudy white heat mark on the board-room table and poured a little of the greyish powder onto it. Then he deftly squeezed a small dab of Squirm into the powder. He rubbed the spot with a soft cloth and there was a gasp of surprise when the heat mark vanished.

"My God!" cried Brashly Crippen, agency V.P. "If it will do that to a table, think of what it will do in your mouth!"

"Exactly!" said young Forthright. "Gentlemen, I think I'm safe in saying that this is the greatest humanitarian discovery since Irium. Three of the four doctors on our staff recommend it. Why, it could even replace teeth!"

Everybody waited now for the Word from Arthur

Coke-Pogue, president of Elongated Toothpaste Corp., the cartel that owned Squirm.

"What do you call that stuff?" Coke-Pogue asked.

"We've decided on the name IDIOP. It's short, functional, and appealing in any language," said Forthright, "but it will also look good on the wrapper. Actually, what we have here is ordinary beach sand: an excellent abrasive."

"It looked like sand," said Coke-Pogue. But he liked the boy's disarming frankness when he lied. "I say we put this program into production at once!"

He was about to signal the end of the conference when a distraught figure burst in waving a newspaper clipping. It was James Whitcomb Heinz, ace agency troubleshooter.

"We're doomed," cried Heinz. "Read this clipping. Toothpaste is obsolete! They've just invented a pill to replace it!" And his body was wracked by great sobs.

A wave of horror rippled down the boardroom table as the awful import of the news made itself felt. Only Wedgwood J. Doggerel refused to take it seriously.

"They'll never go for pills when they can squeeze a tube," he said. "It goes back to prenatal days. The tube is a substitute for their mothers. Our tests show that."

"It won't wash, Doggerel," said Heinz wanly. "This country is pill crazy and we all know it. When they start combining toothpaste pills with tranquilizers, multivitamin capsules, and aspirin, we've had it. Think of it— a pill that cleans your teeth and dulls your mind at the same time, while providing you with valuable nutrition in Nature's Own Way."

As he spoke, several of the agency men present popped tranquilizers into their mouths, so great was their agitation. Then the voice of Coke-Pogue stilled the panic.

"Gentlemen!" cried the great man. "All is not lost. If Squirm can clean teeth, I say it can clean anything. We've had a convincing demonstration here today. Forthright! I want you to launch a subtle campaign at once to convince the public that toothpaste is the greatest natural cleaning agent yet developed. Sneak stuff into the household-hints columns if you have to. Never mind people's teeth. Think of millions of square feet of floors, windows, walls, and coffee tables that need constant attention! I tell you, gentlemen—this is the biggest thing that's hit the industry."

And that's how it began. The rest, of course, is history. It's all in the papers. You could look it up.

GAVIN GRABLEIGH'S NEW IMAGE

Once upon a time there was a fabulously wealthy tycoon named Gavin Grableigh. He owned everything— mines, real estate, factories, hamburger stands, people.

It wasn't true, however, that he had more money than he knew what to do with. He knew exactly what to do with it. He had a swimming pool on his yacht, and on that swimming pool he had *another* yacht. He ate dove eggs poached in champagne for breakfast and filets baked in caviar for lunch. He even had a penthouse in his basement.

He never gave interviews. His rare brace of Snauzzerhunds were trained to eat reporters. In his kitchen he had a gold-plated food processor especially designed to grind up Nikon cameras when photographers ventured too near. He was antisocial, except with women. As a result, everybody hated him.

Indeed, he was hated so much that entire political parties were formed just to denounce him. He didn't care.

One day, Gavin Grableigh was sitting in his giant office atop the ninety-six storey Grableigh Towers examining charts of his various companies. He noted that his Associated Slaveholdings had shown an increased profit, before taxes, of 27 percent on sales, thanks to a slash in the subsistence allowance of the native workers. Grableigh grunted with satisfaction; that was almost as much as the drug companies made. Not only that, Exploitations, Inc., his giant holding company, had trebled its net assets following tax rebates allowed by the new dictator of Anthropodia, whose government was supported entirely by Grableigh money.

But then a muffled curse escaped Grableigh's lips. One of the charts showed a downward trend: Consolidated Inedibles was dropping!

Gavin Grableigh called in his personal executive assistant, who called in *his* personal executive assistant, who had his secretary place a phone call to the secretary of the personal executive assistant of the vice-president in charge of sales for Consolidated Inedibles. After about fifteen minutes of telephone play the two tycoons were connected.

"What's wrong!" barked Gavin Grableigh.

"It's our sales of Slam, the instant-food product that looks, tastes, and acts like salami but is actually manufactured from easy-to-digest, calorie-free cellulose fibre!" cried the harassed vice-president. And he explained that sales were down alarmingly owing to a sinister public relations campaign on behalf of Slur, the rival product in the field. "It's been that way since they hired Russel Sleeth, the smartest public relations man on Madison Avenue!" whimpered the vice-president in charge of sales.

"Then buy Sleeth!" roared Gavin Grableigh. "And have him delivered to me right after lunch." And he was.

"All right, Sleeth," rasped Gavin Grableigh when the two were alone. "What's wrong with Slam?"

"It's what we call image," said Sleeth, casually wiping a speck from the thin slice of his pocket handkerchief. "According to exhaustive motivation-research tests, the public just can't stand Slam's image."

"What *is* Slam's image?"

"You."

"Me?"

"Yes. They connect you with Slam. They hate you; ergo, they hate Slam."

"Then change the name. Call it Slop or something."

"No good. Your competitors have got on to something. They'll always link any of your products with your image and your sales will plummet."

"But this is serious, Sleeth! What do we do?"

"Easy, Mr. Grableigh. We change *your* image."

Thus began the great campaign to make Gavin Grableigh loved by all the people. Russel Sleeth asked only one boon: if he succeeded he wanted the hand of Gavin Grableigh's daughter, Griselda, in marriage. Gavin Grableigh quickly agreed.

The campaign began slowly, then built steam: at first nothing more than a few shots for *Gracious Living* magazine showing Grableigh puttering in his garden and cooking a mess of vichyssoise on his charcoal burner;

then a spattering of warm, folksy articles, such as "Gavin Grableigh, Misunderstood Tycoon" and "The Vision of Gavin Grableigh," began to appear, followed by first-person pieces, such as "My Ten Easy Rules for Success," by Gavin Grableigh, "How Prayer Made Me Ten Million Dollars," by Gavin Grableigh, "Gavin Grableigh's Formula for Instant Happiness," "What Lent Means to Me," and many others.

This was only the beginning. Gavin Grableigh was soon in heavy demand as a public speaker, fundraiser, cultural arbiter, and panel moderator—as were his bright young men. Grableigh Manor was thrown open for symphony teas and hospital garden parties. Grableigh executives appeared on boards of hospitals, universities, and money-losing projects. During Heart Fund Week a vice-president personally had a heart attack as an example to the nation and during the final days of the cancer drive another of Grableigh's lieutenants got cancer to show that it could be cured.

Two years to the day after Russel Sleeth began his campaign, Gavin Grableigh was named Citizen of the Year, retroactive for two years. The sales of Slam hit a new high.

The following day Gavin Grableigh called Russel Sleeth into his office. "You've destroyed my organization," he said. "You're fired!"

It was true. Grableigh's first vice-president was now spending all his time in a tuxedo at the Grableigh Centre for the Performing Arts. His second vice-president was working round the clock selecting adjudicators for the drama festival. His third vice-president was in England receiving a conservation award because the Grableigh Conservation Club had saved the red-breasted harbinger from extinction. All the junior executives were out being community leaders, raising funds for memorial arenas, attending Boy Scout camp, and making speeches about Elmer the Safety Elephant.

"There's nobody left to mind the store!" shouted Grableigh. "Besides, if I have to eat one more Hilton Hotel luncheon I'll go mad. Take my daughter and get out—she's a dog anyway."

And he called the Volunteer Rehabilitation Centre, got his personal executive assistant out of the basket-weaving class, and ordered him to poach a filet in caviar.

"I'd rather be hated," said Gavin Grableigh, munching away greedily.

Russel Sleeth didn't care. Griselda *was* a dog, as it turned out, but she certainly had a lot of important contacts.

THE GREAT DETERGENT PREMIUM RACE

The idea was born in the mind of J. Algernon Krief, a junior account executive with the advertising agency of Carstairs, Moulton, Wary, Winnow, Finch, Booster, and Quail; but it was stolen almost at once by the executive vice-president, Edward DeLancy Strainge.

Young Krief had worked for several years on the Drudge account. As you remember, Drudge was the all-purpose cleanser that banished washday drudgery, made your dishes sparkle like new, helped you bid farewell to Blue Monday nerves, brought back life to tired eyes, made clothes bluer than blue, ended laundry-tub wrinkles, contained lanolin, and reduced stomach acidity. There was a slogan about Drudge taking out the drudgery, and a singing commercial about never bearing a grudge, and a lot more jazz like that.

Well, J. Algernon Krief, who had been just plain Joe Krief until he became a junior account executive, was put to work on the Drudge account, premium division.

At first it was pretty simple. The firm printed a coupon on the box top and if you saved ten of these, and if they were all the right colour, and if you mailed them in with two dollars in coin or stamps you received a genuine silver-plated egg-shirrer in the beautiful Carleton design, worth at least $2.49 in any retail store.

This was a mild success. It caused a flurry of coupon trading among housewives and enough extra Drudge was sold to make husbands complain of a soapy taste on their butter knives. But then the makers of Drab, sensing competition, went Drudge one better.

Drab, you'll recall, was the sensational new washday miracle discovery that removed drabness from everyday life, contained an amazing new scientific suds ingredient (Radiant-5), produced rich, abundant lather, made pots and pans gleam like jewels, was kind to your skin, and brought, fast, fast, fast relief. I forgot to say that its gentle soothing action did wonders with laces and fine fabrics. The makers of Drab printed a coupon on their box that, all by itself, was good for a genuine nickel-plated olive mincer, the kind used by many glamorous Hollywood stars. This valuable premium was rushed to your door for a mere ten cents in stamps or coins to cover packaging and mailing.

The Drudge people fought back fiercely. Soon the supermarket shelves were jammed with boxes of Drudge in the exciting new flip-top package, heralding the fact that no coupon at all was needed to secure a beautiful solid chromium, hand-engraved quince parer, designed by Raymond Loewy. One of these useful implements was actually attached to the side of each box of Drudge.

As a result, so much Drudge was sold that, in a single Vancouver suburb, eighteen septic-tank repairmen were able to take expensive six-week vacations in Hawaii.

The Drab company did not take this lying down. They put their next premium—a beautifully hand-tooled stainless-steel nutmeg grater—*inside* the box, mixed up with the Drab.

This had several advantages. For one thing there was the thrilling sense of discovery when the housewife, on shaking quantities of Drab into the automatic washer, suddenly spotted the nutmeg grater churning about among the nylon panties. Then there was the fact that the nutmeg grater actually replaced some of the Drab. The company had less to make, the housewife had less to get rid of. And that was how J. Algernon Krief, whose friends (alas) still called him Joe, got his great idea.

Young Krief was a man obsessed with charts, graphs, surveys in depth, door-to-door polls, motivational studies, and tests. It was he, for instance, who discovered that the placing of *two* premiums, rather than one, in a box of Drudge increased the angle of the sales graph by 17.4 degrees during the months of December and March.

Emboldened, Krief decided to test *three* premiums per box in eight selected cities for a period of five weeks. These premiums were: (1) a genuine zircon solitaire stick-pin in a simulated 14-karat-gold mounting, which gave an air of success and affluence to all who wore it (for the man of the house); (2) two giant-sized Howitzer-brand bath towels, labelled MADAME and MONSIEUR (for the housewife); and (3) an automatic Zap gun, which threw a real flame fifty feet (for the children).

These premiums, stuffed into enormous Drudge boxes, dominated the supermarkets and boosted the sale of Drudge by 512.3 percent in the test cities. Even more significant, a greater number of stickpins, towels, and Zap guns were sold in this way than in the normal way through retail stores.

But Krief discovered something far more significant: though sales were up, *the actual quantity of Drudge being manufactured had dropped.* Some of the vats were only half full. The reason was simple enough: there just wasn't very much room left in the Drudge cartons for Drudge.

As I say, this idea was stolen at once by the executive vice-president, but there's no denying its revolutionary effect on the soap and detergent business.

The Drudge Company, by firing all its research chemists, statistically reduced its overhead. Housewives were delighted to find the Drudge packages jammed with premiums. It was like Christmas every day to buy Drudge. And the graphs proved that the sales of Drudge had increased by 1013.4 percent—even though none was being made.

Drab followed suit instantly and the entire industry swiftly swung into line. Soon other companies began boosting their own sales with premiums. In fact, even the premiums had premiums. A packaged-rice firm, for example, gave away boxes of Cracker Jack, which themselves contained premiums.

But it remained for the Howitzer Towel Company to reach the peak of premium giving. One of its bright young men conceived the idea of giving away soap with each towel sold. Then as the idea caught on, packages of detergent, such as Drudge.

Drudge, meanwhile, was giving away Howitzer towels by the millions. Which meant if you wanted a Howitzer towel you bought Drudge, and if you wanted Drudge you bought a Howitzer towel, and everything was the same as before. Only the names were changed to confuse the innocent.

A LITTLE DAB'LL DO IT

*N**ow, now, Mr. Garson, just lie quietly there on the couch while I make some notes. You say you're having this trouble with women?*

That's right, Doctor. It's just about driving me out of my mind.

Exactly what is the trouble, Mr. Garson?

Well, I no sooner leave the house in the morning than it begins. Women jump out and practically attack me on the street. They nuzzle up against me on the subway, running their fingers through my hair and cooing in my ear. I have to carry a set of golf clubs to beat off the secretaries when I reach the office. I find a Number Two iron very effective for the purpose.

When did you first notice this phenomenon?

Just three days ago, Doctor. It began on the morning of Friday, November 13.

I think you'd better give a pretty detailed account of your actions on that particular morning. When you arose to face the day was there any change in the normal cycle of events?

Not that I can recall. I shaved, of course, savouring the soothing mentholated lather of delicious double rich Top Whip, the instant shaving cream that contains the mysterious chemical ingredient J-107, an amazing discovery that automatically cleans as it polishes. I set the complicated dials of my new superspeed razor (styled to my personal convenience) to position 22 and enjoyed one of the cleanest shaves a man ever had. After that was done, I shaved my hidden beard together with a small peach that my wife offered me for breakfast, using my new three-speed electric razor for which I have just recently received full engineer's papers. Man, oh, man, doctor, there's nothing like a clean fresh shave to set you up in the morning and start you off feeling refreshed.

Yes, of course, Garson, but this was simply normal practice with you, I take it.

Normal! I'll say it's normal. Why, shaving's a downright joy since I've got my—

Yes, yes, Garson, but let's go on with your story. I don't feel that we've got to the bottom of the mystery yet. What happened next?

Well, Doctor, I'm the sort of guy who just isn't able to brush his teeth three times a day. That's why I'm fortunate in being able to fall back on new blue Swill, the miracle mouth detergent that guards tooth enamel up to twenty-four hours after a single brushing in nine out of fourteen cases tested. Swill isn't a paste, isn't a cream either. It's what your dentist uses: millions of tiny grains of pure sand. And because it contains a secret ingredient *metatarsal,* it gives double the lasting protection of inferior brand B while leaving your mouth morning-fresh and your teeth gleaming white. Man, it was certainly a red-letter day for me when Grebe Franistatch persuaded me to switch to Swill.

You brushed your teeth, that's what you're trying to say, is it, Garson?

Doctor, when you use Swill you do more than just "brush your teeth." You actually encase the living enamel with a protective screen of—

Exactly. But I don't think this is at the root of your problem. What did you do next?

Well, Doctor, a man can't be too careful about his personal habits. Now, I know that most men think that underarm deodorants are sissified, but that's because they haven't tried Gruff, the new all-purpose deodorant for men only. Because it's scented with a subtle blend of fine tobaccos, Gruff has that he-man quality most deodorants lack. And it's so easy to use, too! Just a gentle click of Gruff's exclusive push-button dial, adjusted by skilled engineers to your personal setting, and you've got twenty-four-hour medicated protection. Gruff not only saves bathing but it's guaranteed to contain no lanolin, another plus factor from the famous laboratories of—

All right, Garson, I've got the message. How long have you been using Gruff?

Twenty-one days now, Doctor, and would you believe it?—the generous, economy-size bottle is still giving me full-strength service at the click of the button.

Then that isn't the clue to your problem, either. Garson,

I'm going to be blunt with you. I have the feeling you're keeping something back from me.

But, Doctor, I'm trying to be completely frank.

No doubt you believe you are. But deep in your sub-conscious you're concealing something. It's my task to discover it. Now, Garson, I notice a suspiciously healthy sheen to your hair; I might even say it was "disturbingly healthy"—

It was only a little dab, Doctor. I didn't think it was worth mentioning.

A little dab will do it, Garson. That's the trouble with you joy-poppers. You don't understand you're playing with fire.

But I wanted my hair to have that well-groomed feeling, Doctor. I was tired of greasy hair lotions that gave me that slicked-down appearance. I wanted to look so debonair. I didn't realize the girls would all pursue me if I simply rubbed a little in my hair.

Watch this simple demonstration, Garson, and I think it will convince you this is no ordinary hair lotion. I'm standing in front of a machine similar to those developed by the armed forces for testing the reaction of women to ordinary infantry soldiers in the field. Now watch closely while I place a tube of Inferior Hair Oil "B" against the sensitive mechanism. Notice that the dial hardly quivers. Now give me that tube you're secretly clutching in your hand. I take the tiniest dab, place it in front of the machine—and watch that dial leap! There's proof positive, Garson, that you have been toying with the most powerful aphrodisiac known to man!

Gee, Doc, and here all the time I thought it was just another hair oil. Man, oh, man, it certainly was a red-letter day for me when I walked into your office. Thanks to you I can throw away my golf clubs!

Glad to be of service, Mr. Garson. And now you must excuse me. I have a particularly difficult case awaiting me. Young woman suffering from strange Freudian dreams. Sees herself walking down the Champs-Elysées, meeting Khrushchev, appearing on fixed quiz shows, et cetera, clad only in her bra. We call it the Maidenform Syndrome.

THE FIRST TV EXECUTION

The execution was originally scheduled for dawn, but was changed to eight-thirty in the evening because the sponsor insisted on a peak viewing time. Some of the boys in the agency said that it could be put on videotape with no loss of quality, but the account executives said no, dammit, the great thing about doing an execution on TV was that you were doing it "live," so to speak.

So eight-thirty it was, Sunday night, right after church and not so late that the kiddies would miss the proceedings, which were highly educational and devoted to the proposition that Crime Does Not Pay. The producer planned generous acknowledgements to the sponsors of *Murder, She Wrote*—for relinquishing their time so the execution might be televised.

Nobody thought to thank Roger Mahaffy for relinquishing his life, so the show might go on, but then Roger Mahaffy did not count for much. In the whole one-hour spectacle he was the only one who had no lines to learn. He had murdered his wife with a blunt instrument in a fit of passion, and the whole show was designed to prevent other husbands from murdering their wives in subsequent fits of passion.

The idea of televising a real execution had been greeted with enthusiasm by press, public, and government leaders when it was first broached, with great dignity, by the Green, Garston, Fullmer, Blight & Leach advertising agency. You may recall that a few years before, certain milksops, interested in only coddling criminals, had urged the abolition of the death penalty. They were roundly and rightly denounced by civic leaders who pointed out, first, that a criminal ought to pay for his crime and, second, that the death penalty acted as a strong deterrent against further crimes of the same sort. Without the example of The Chair, they said, the streets would not be safe for honest men.

This was the exact point made by Barton J. Leach, the most powerful advertising man in America. Capital punishment *was* a deterrent, he said, just like the atomic bomb. And it could be a much greater deterrent if it was brought home to millions of citizens at a peak viewing time. Why should it be carried out in secret in the dark of the night behind prison walls? Were we ashamed of it, or something? And why should it be a continual burden on the taxpayer when there were commercial men of vision willing to pick up the tab and, in addition, to pay the government a neat profit?

These arguments were more than convincing, especially when Barton J. Leach announced that the agency would make sure that a high-class sponsor would be found and that the proceedings would be carried out with great dignity. Dignity, indeed, was to be the keynote of the entire affair.

When the sponsor was revealed, press and public agreed that the execution could scarcely be carried out under more dignified auspices. The credentials of the Gainsborough Brewers and Distillers Corp. were impeccable. Their long-term interest in conservation, their sponsorship of the Gainsborough Ballet, their well-known travelling exhibitions of American art, their backing of the Gainsborough Philharmonic, the Middlebrow (Pa.) Festival of the Arts, and the Grey Cup—all these philanthropies, together with the well-known fact that their products were consumed exclusively by graduates of Harvard, ensured that no motives of sordid commercialism would enter the picture. There would be a brief and tastefully animated cartoon of dancing beer mugs, nothing more.

Walter Cronkite came out of retirement to act as the Voice of Gainsborough, delivering the public service announcements that the company planned in lieu of normal commercials. These were moral pronouncements about Life to the Full, Enjoying Life While You Can, Drink the Cup of Life's Fulfilment to the Final Drop, and so on.

A monsignor, a deacon, and a rabbi were engaged to give nondenominational religious messages on the essential evils of crime and to point out, in addition, that people who committed murder usually got burned for it. Nobody bothered to ask the prisoner's religion, which, as it happened, was Zen Buddhist.

The make-up girls arrived at six-thirty and made up the warden, the priests, the guards, and the executioner. They used a special No. 4 Max Factor pancake on the prisoner to hide his unearthly pallor. Otherwise, as they told him chattily, his face would burn right out under the lights.

The condemned man was given a hearty dinner just before the program began. He had actually eaten at five-thirty and wasn't hungry, but the agency had thought it would be a nice touch to show him polishing off a fried chicken at the top of the show. There were credits for McDonald's, which supplied the food, and also for Canadian Airlines International, which flew the executioner in.

The makeshift studio presented a busy sight as the time of execution drew near, and some of the sponsor's guests, who had never been on the inside of a real TV performance before, were very impressed by its efficiency.

The camera crew had already had three dry and one live rehearsal in the chamber itself. There were cue cards for everybody except the prisoner. The executioner went through his bit in rehearsal several times before the producer was satisfied: there was a tendency to rush things and, in TV, as the producer kept saying over and over again, timing is everything. This was one show they wanted to come out on cue.

One of the agency's bright boys had invented a nice piece of business and it worked excellently. A hidden announcer talked about the possibility of a last-minute reprieve, saying that the lawyers had uncovered new evidence and the governor was considering the matter as the show began. This was fiction, of course. You can bet that on an execution as important as this one there wasn't going to be any slip-up. But it did add the element of suspense that is so important in shows of this kind.

Well, I needn't describe the actual show. You saw it all, as I did, and you know how successful it was. All the critics gave it raves, and the ratings surpassed even the agency's wildest expectations. The prisoner might have acted a little better, there, towards the middle of the show; but then, as Barton J. Leach said, this one was only a sort of pilot production. On future shows—and you can bet there'll be plenty more—that sort of detail will be smartly taken care of.

MUSICAL INTERLUDE

WAR AND PEACE!
WAR AND PEACE!
MY LOVE FOR YOU
WILL NEVER CEASE!

The practice of taking movie titles and turning them into popular songs to advance box office sales as well as records is well established in Hollywood. From *The Sound of Music* to *Pretty Woman*, the titles that fit the marquees have, with the help of matching lyrics and sprightly tunes, consistently made the *Billboard* charts.

This has been more than galling to Roland Carstairs, who thought up the idea but has received no credit for it. Carstairs's problem may be that he didn't think of putting movie titles to work as pop numbers; he concentrated, instead, on book titles, with lamentable results. The publishers of William Shirer's massive tome *The Rise and Fall of the Third Reich* turned up their noses at this offering:

The Rise and Fall of the Third Reich
Was nothing compared to our love;

Our romance took off like a motorbike
Blessed by the Heavens above.
Then it suddenly faltered,
It rose and it fell
Just like
The Third Reich
It didn't do so well.
So now you know, darling,
Just what I feel like;
My heart has been broken
Like the famous Third Reich.

He had no success, either, with John Gunther's *Inside Europe Today*, though many of his fans felt it was his masterpiece:

Inside Europe Today
There's a girl with a love that's new;
Inside Europe Today
There's a girl with a heart that's true!
(LOUDER) How can I reach her?
She's got so much pride!
For she's Inside Europe Today
And I'm trapped outside!

Carstairs was certain that an all-out advertising campaign using John Galbraith's *Affluent Society* as a song title would put the book on the *New York Times* best-seller list. Hollywood would have jumped at these lyrics, and it takes nothing away from Carstairs to note that the book made the best-seller list anyway.

The Affluent Society
Is not my dish of tea
In moments of sobriety
All that I want—is thee!
I have a funny feeling
That our love is Heaven-sent.
To me you're real Society
Though you're not Affluent.

Carstairs felt that a strongly scored lyric of the popular hurtin' type might easily revive sagging sales of Thorstein Veblen's classic tome *The Theory of the Leisure Class*:

You gave me a love
That I cannot measure.
You gave me a mem'ry
That I'll always treasure.
For you had the Class
And I had the Leisure,
And that's why I'm cry-in' for you! (SOB)
My heart's hanging heavy,
My soul stands debased,
Oh, please come back, baby,
Please come back in haste!
I've broken the Law
Of Conspicuous Waste
Because I've been cry-in' for you! (SOB)
Yes, I'm cry-in' for you!
I'm cry-in' for you!
My life is incredibly dreary.

For you torment my Leisure
With memories of pleasure:
If you love me, it's only in Theory.

Now, after a hiatus of some years, Carstairs is back
at it. He recently approached Garth Drabinsky with a
title song for his autobiography, *Closer to the Sun*. But
Drabinsky, in spite of his close links with show business,
would have none of it, explaining that the book's bud-
get had been squandered on such foolish gimmicks as
launching parties and bookstore autographings.

Whenever I kiss you
I feel closer to the sun,
Whenever I miss you
I know you're the one.
Please tell me it's my turn
To bask in your rays,
I want to be sunburned
For the rest of my days.
What will I do when the sun sets
And December takes over from June?
How can I live in the twilight
With my only companion, the Moon?
Oh, baby, please warm me
When daylight is done,
Because even at midnight
I feel closer to the sun.

Nor did Timothy Findley, himself a man of the theatre,
demonstrate any enthusiasm when Carstairs showed

him the treatment he had in mind to promote Findley's latest success, *The Piano Man's Daughter.*

She was just a Piano Man's Daughter,
But she played on the strings of my heart,
And when she applied the soft pedal
I knew we were fated to part.
In a silken chemise
She fingered my keys
But that was the end of our *sortie.*
I tried hard to please
But she gave me the freeze
Because my response was too *forte.*
And now as I sit in the gloaming
And sip a thin whiskey and water
I dream of the lovely concerto
I played with the Piano Man's Daughter.

Just the other day Carstairs made one final pitch to Stoddart Publishing to boost sales of Stevie Cameron's *On the Take* with what he considered a brilliant torch song:

I wooed you with diamonds
And vintage champagne,
I took you to Paris
On a jet aeroplane.
I brought you from nowhere,
Put meat on your table,
I leased you a Lexus
And clothed you in sable.

Yet you won't adore me
And I feel my heart break,
I'm on my knees, baby,
But *you're* on the take.

Spurned by another Canadian publisher! Carstairs took it hard. Still, as he said, what can you expect from a timid, stick-in-the-mud industry that suffers habitually from an inferiority complex?

Well, one publisher—the one whose name appears on this slim volume—decided to bite the bullet. Driven almost batty by an inability to devise any method to shore up sagging sales, the company gave Carstairs *carte blanche* to produce a winner that would cause people to burst into book shops carolling the title.

It might well have worked, but Carstairs, in his moment of triumph, was brought down by his rhyming dictionary. Search as he might, he was never able to find a word to rhyme with *Century*.

Four

POPULAR CULTURE AS WE KNEW IT

Lord, heap miseries upon us
yet entwine our arts with laughters low!
James Joyce

DOESN'T JAMES BOND REALIZE NO MEANS NO?

M'Lud, the next item on the court docket is a triple charge of sexual harassment against one James Bond, who lists his occupation simply as "Spy." May I outline the prosecution's case?

Thank you, M'Lud. The first incident involves a young woman aviator, bearing the unfortunate name of Pussy Galore. The evidence, which has been gathered by a private investigative body known as SPECTRE, is quite conclusive, having been captured on film.

The assault took place in a building on a farm of a well-known businessman, a certain Mr. Goldfinger. The accused, Bond, attempted to subdue Miss Galore by the use of Oriental martial arts, but the plucky young woman fought back.

Having failed at strong-arm methods, he attempted to bribe her. "What would it take for you to see things my way?" he propositioned. But she refused any offer. "A lot more than you've got!" she told him.

It is clear that she wanted nothing to do with this libertine, yet he persisted. "Isn't it customary to grant the condemned man his last request?" he asked her with a leer. To which the virtuous Miss Galore made her position clear. "Get out!" she told him.

But the lecherous Bond apparently doesn't believe that "no" actually means "No!" He flung her onto a pile of straw, and though she attempted to fight him off, he had his way with her.

Thanks to more admirable sleuthing by SPECTRE, we also have film of another unwanted sexual encounter between this unregenerate debaucher and a young masseuse named Pat. We have it filed under the code name THUNDERBALL. The incident took place in a private health clinic where, as is clear from the film, Bond could not keep his hands off her.

"Behave yourself," she told him firmly, but realized that the only way to forestall his unwanted attention was to confine him in a machine, "the only place to keep you quiet."

Later, she sent him into the steam room in another attempt to slow his ardour. "It might even shrink you down to size," she said. As the film shows, her meaning was quite clear.

But that was not the end. The wicked Bond knew that Pat would be in trouble with her boss if she told him what was going on. "You wouldn't tell Dr. Gray," she pleaded. "Please, I'd lose my job."

M'Lud, the callous Bond didn't give a hoot about her job. He wanted her body and was determined to get it through blackmail. "I suppose my silence could have a price," he leered.

The film shows that he made a grab for her and that she resisted, moaning, "Oh no! Oh no!" "Oh yes!" cried the evil Bond, who again refused to believe that "No!" means just that. Again, he had his way with her.

I now turn your attention to the file—code named LIVE AND LET DIE. This scene, again secretly filmed by the SPECTRE operative, is enough to leave a stench in the nostrils of any decent man or woman.

In this incident, the swinish Bond worked his will on a young and innocent virgin by employing the crassest and most devious form of deception. The young woman in question, one Solitaire, is an expert tarot card reader, a profession that apparently requires celibacy.

Because she pulled a card titled The Lovers, Bond insisted she was destined to bed him. "The cards say you must," he explained.

When she demurred, he produced a fresh pack of cards and asked her to pick one. To her dismay she again picked The Lovers. What she didn't know was that this defiler of women had stacked the deck so *every card was the same*.

"Come, darling," he hissed. "There has to be a first time for everything."

She felt herself helpless. The gods, she believed, had compelled her to earthly love and taken away her powers. As she put it, "Physical violation cannot be undone."

And, of course, physical violation followed.

The prosecution rests its case, M'Lud.

"SPY" JAILED FOR SEX ATTACKS
London (AP)—A so-called spy, Commander James

Bond of the Royal Navy, was sentenced to six years in prison today after filmed evidence showed he had committed unwanted sexual assaults on three young women.

A Miss Moneypenny, who identified herself as a secretary, appeared for the defence, testifying that Bond had never laid a hand on her, a fact, she said, she had always regretted.

Several young women who created a disturbance in the gallery were evicted by the court.

THE ULTIMATE WINE TASTING

The century was more than half over before the wine snobs took charge. Before that time wine had been manufactured almost exclusively for people who drank it in doorways. Cheap sherry was the plonk of choice, although the occasional straw-covered bottle of bad Chianti was seen gracing an upper-class table, or, on festive occasions, a kind of alcoholic pop known as Sparkling Burgundy.

Then everything changed. People began to "discover" little-known wines and to lord it over their friends. Men who would turn up their noses at a flagon of blackberry juice now began to discover a whiff of blackberries in the "finish" of certain Burgundies. Wine and cheese parties—bad wine, worse cheese—became the rage. Wine clubs blossomed. Wine experts became minor deities.

These experts attended wine tastings, which were held regularly. There, the high priests of the wine trade talked learnedly of each wine's "nose," its complexity, its body, its depth, its finish. They sipped the wine, rolled it around on their tongues, savoured it. *But they didn't drink it.* Instead, they spit it out into a pail and went on to taste the next wine offered.

This did not sit well with Stefan G. Vronsky, a wine lover and small-time vintner. "It's all right to babble on about nose, finish, and character," he'd say. "But what about *buzz?* If there's no buzz, who cares about character?"

Vronsky decided to organize a series of wine tastings to which all the leading experts were invited. But at his tasting no one would be allowed to spit out the wine; they *had to swallow it.*

It was a memorable occasion, the first of these new-type wine tastings. Seventy wines were offered, including a rare Châteaux Margaux, which any wine lover would kill for, and a '29 Lafite. Each expert was allowed a little bread and mild cheese on which to nibble between tastings as he scribbled its qualities on a special form before quaffing it.

The tasting proceeded without incident until the seventh wine sample—a two-ounce mouthful. At that point, the venerable critic for the *Wine Spectator* smacked his lips and was heard to shout: "Through the teeth and over the gums! Look out, stomach, here it comes!"

A murmur of approval rippled through the company, causing the author of *Wine and Civilization* to toss back his portion in a gulp and ask for seconds.

On the eleventh sampling, the wine editor of *Gourmet* got into a verbal squabble with the author of *What Wine Means to Me,* not about wine but about whether there was a personal God who could influence the course of human affairs.

On the fourteenth sample, the wine critic for *Soldier of Fortune* joined the discussion by attempting to quote from Kierkegaard but found he was no longer able to pronounce the name.

On the seventeenth sample, the author of *The Magic of Burgundy* fell asleep, while the wine columnist for the *Wall Street Journal* offered to fight anybody in the room.

On the twentieth sample, the chief columnist for *Wine Education* began to sing: "She's got hair on her belly like the branches of a tree." The managing editor of *Popular Vintages* joined in.

On the twenty-fourth sample, the wine columnist for *Good Parenting* found he could make no sense of his scribbled record. Against the word "nose," for instance, he had written "runny." This caused him to convulse with laughter. After that he tore up his card. "It's all nonsense," he said. "Lesh give every wine an 89!"

Those who were still standing chorused agreement. Only Stefan G. Vronsky demurred. He was, you'll probably remember, the only wine maker in all of Saskatchewan, and his Château Batoche was truly memorable for its buzz, if not its complexity.

"You've got to taste this," he said, pouring a generous quantity of Château Batoche for each of the assembly, including the ones on the floor. "I think you'll agree that this, more than any other, has the quality a great wine requires: *buzz!*"

A chorus of cheers greeted this announcement as each expert tossed back his Château Batoche with a single gulp.

"Wow!" cried the editor of the *Wine Circular.*

"Whoopee!" shouted the columnist for *Rare Vintages* just before he slid noiselessly to the floor.

It was agreed that all the wines at the tasting, including several that had not been tasted, would be awarded a coveted 89, except for the Château Batoche, which received a 91.

Vronsky was delighted. His ads now offered "Wine with a Buzz." With the loosening of legal structures, Château Batoche can now be purchased at leading hardware stores at a modest price. They say it makes the perfect companion to well-charred beef.

NEW BROADCAST RULES FROM THE CRTC

The Canadian Radio-television and Telecommunications Commission has just issued a set of approved questions and responses for use in radio and TV on-the-spot interviews during the upcoming season. The board warns that it will continue its policy of monitoring stations; interviewers and interviewees using questions or answers not on the approved list will be called to account.

A new set of questions and answers has been approved for the use of on-the-spot interviewers with beauty contest winners. These apply to all levels of beauty contests, starting with the Miss Women's Institute of Gravenhurst contest and running right up to the coveted Mr. and Mrs. Typical Canadian Couple Contest.

APPROVED QUESTION 1: Well, (*first name of winner here*), how does it feel to be named Miss (*name of contest here*) of 1995?

APPROVED ANSWER 1: Feels pretty wonderful. It's just the most wonderful thing that's ever happened.

APPROVED QUESTION 2: Feels pretty wonderful, eh?

APPROVED ANSWER 2: Oh, it's just—you have no idea how wonderful.

APPROVED QUESTION 3: Would you say this is the greatest day of your life?

APPROVED ANSWER 3: Yes, definitely. This is the greatest day of my life. It's just wonderful.

APPROVED QUESTION 4: Did you think you were going to be chosen the winner when you first entered the contest?

APPROVED ANSWER 4: No, I honestly didn't. It was such a surprise because I really didn't think I had a chance with all these other wonderful contestants.

APPROVED QUESTION 5: It was a real surprise, then, eh?

APPROVED ANSWER 5: It really was a surprise. A real surprise.

APPROVED QUESTION 6: How does your mother feel about all this?

APPROVED ANSWER 6: Oh, she just thinks it's pretty wonderful.

APPROVED QUESTION 7: And the rest of your family? How do they feel? Do they think it's wonderful, too?

APPROVED ANSWER 7: They think it's just wonderful!

APPROVED QUESTION 8: So now that you're Miss (*name of contest here*), what are your plans for the future?

APPROVED ANSWER 8: My only desire is to justify the faith in me of all the wonderful people who voted for me and rooted for me. They've been just wonderful.

The CRTC has approved a Standard Closing for interviews with beauty contest winners and warns that announcers departing from the Standard Closing will be dealt with severely.

STANDARD CLOSING: Well, thank you, Cheryl Ann (*or other name if name is not Cheryl Ann*). You've been a really wonderful contestant and a credit to your community, and I know I speak for your friends and everybody when I say we wish you all the luck in the world for whatever the future holds.

The commission has also noticed some laxity seeping into the comments of baseball and football announcers when turning microphones over to their colleagues. It again points out that standard procedure for this was developed during the 1936 World Series and has not changed since:

FIRST ANNOUNCER: And now it's come time to turn over the old microphone to my good friend and sidekick (*name here*), a wonderful sportscaster and a really great guy—and I mean that sincerely—who will be detailing the rest of the play for you with his customary skill.

SECOND ANNOUNCER: Well thank you (*name here*) for those very kind words which I appreciate sincerely and I just want to say what a pleasure it always is to work the series with yourself.

Drill has now been standardized for on-the-spot interviews with onlookers lining the streets at *all* parades, whether these be Santa Claus, Grey Cup, Orangemen's, or other. Detail can be found in section 27 of the Board's book of regulations. Under the new procedure, only one question is now to be asked: "What do you think of the parade?" The procedure has been simplified because, for the past three years, this has been the only question asked anyway.

The Board has ruled that the question may be preceded by one of several Approved Comments, listed in subsection (j). For instance, the Approved Comment for boys under ten is: "Here's a young fella looks like he's having a grand time."

Slight variations in answers, however, are allowed to the Approved Question "What do you think of the parade?" These are: (1) I think it's really wonderful. (2) Great. (3) It's really wonderful.

The same set of questions and answers may now be used for on-the-spot interviews after election results are known. However, it is important for announcers to remember that the word "election" must be substituted for "parade" when talking to the Man on the Street.

The following Approved Statement has been standardized for losing candidates at political conventions.

APPROVED STATEMENT: The delegates have made their wishes felt in no uncertain terms, and I am happy to approve that decision. If there have been differences of opinion here they have been differences of method, not of basic goals. After all, the thing to remember is that we are all loyal (*name of political affiliation here*). We have only one aim: victory in (*date of next election here*)! The time has come for this great party to close ranks behind the man who will be the next (*name of political office here*) and get on with the job. Speaking for myself, I intend to work twenty-four hours a day, seven days a week, for the successful election of your choice and mine—(*name of winning nominee here*).

Certain basic changes have been made in the Standard Invoking-the-Deity response to Approved Question 7 for boxing and wrestling champions and winning Olympic hockey coaches.

APPROVED QUESTION: Looking back on it now, who do you credit for your big win?

APPROVED ANSWER: Well, Mel, I know this sounds a little strange coming from a guy like me, but I don't think I coulda done it without God's help.

Students of the CRTC handbook will note that the Standard Response to Approved Question 36 in disc jockey interviews with stars of stage, screen, or TV remains unchanged.

APPROVED QUESTION: Looking back on it now, what's the biggest factor in your success?

APPROVED ANSWER: Well, Gil, let's just say I've been awfully, awfully lucky.

Recently a celebrity, in replying to this question, stated that he had reached his present state of success by sheer pluck and hard work. The station's licence is being suspended for six weeks.

RALPH JASPER'S PUBLISHING TRIUMPH

My friend Ralph Jasper has gone into the magazine business, and this time I think he's come up with a real winner.

I know, I know: it's not a great time to be a publisher. Advertising is down, magazines are getting thinner, newspapers and television get the story faster. Nonetheless, Ralph is prospering because he has latched on to a unique idea. That's how great publishers are born.

It came to Ralph after reading an item in the press about the disciplining of Dr. Zoltan Znabolwisc, a well-known dental practitioner. Maybe you saw it.

Znabolwisc was reprimanded by the Canadian Dental Ethics Association because, it was discovered, he was carrying up-to-date magazines in his waiting room. Some were only two or three months old and several still had their covers.

The wretched Znabolwisc, sensing that the jig was up, tried to conceal a recent issue of *National Furnishings* under a three-year-old copy of *Business Trends*. But the inspectors caught him in the act, and now Znabolwisc has suffered ostracism.

Ralph Jasper, apparently, is the only entrepreneur to seize the moment and exploit the misfortune of others like Znabolwisc, who may, without knowing it, have new publications concealed in their magazine racks. He decided at once to fill a need and publish a series of old, boring magazines, suitably worn and tattered, with pages missing, for professional waiting rooms across the nation.

He delivers to each subscriber—dentist, doctor, optometrist, whatever—a package of ten publications every two months. These range from such old waiting-room favourites as *The Cattle Breeder's Monthly* to more "popular" publications with vague names like *Verve* or *Spiel*.

One really obscure publication is called *Smurdge*. Nobody, including Ralph, knows what it's about. It mainly contains photographs of unsmiling businessmen in dark suits, lifted and rephotographed from the financial pages of old daily newspapers, which, in Robert Benchley's immortal words, seem to have been engraved on bread.

Ralph has been especially successful with the professional publications that he has produced. Anybody who has twiddled his thumbs in a doctor's outside office is surely familiar with the genre. But Ralph has improved mightily on the originals.

His professional magazines, *The Canadian Medical Examiner*, *The Journal of the Poughkeepsie Optometrists Association*, *Modern Orthodontistry*—contain far more charts and graphs than is usual, thus making the articles totally incomprehensible to the laymen in the waiting rooms.

Ralph loves to use buzzwords that suggest to the unwashed that the professions have their own mysterious language. A great word is "incidence," as in "Incidence of Retraction among Female Subjects, between ages of 12 and 32, during downhill phase of Rackenstantrum's Syndrome."

Ralph is also a great believer in footnotes—the kind that will stop any unwary patient in his tracks if he tries to work his way through, say, *The Glaucoma Monthly*. Ralph's footnotes take up more space than the article itself, and are printed in type so small that the frustrated reader who gets that far will automatically be softened up for a new pair of lenses.

Ralph takes pride in giving his professional publications a well-thumbed look, getting across the idea that the man in the white coat is keeping up with the latest advances in science. Ralph thumbs these magazines himself before they are put through the tattering machine.

As you can imagine, the response has been gratifying.

Dr. Waverly B. Seminal writes: "The March 1979 issue of *The Pennsylvania Journal of Dental Caries* was just jim-dandy. I especially liked the piece on 'The Ten Top Orthodontists in Scranton.' I scarcely needed to use Novocain after that one."

Dr. Ephraim Koshevoy, the well-known ophthalmologist, waxes enthusiastic about Jasper's latest offering, *The Garbage Disposal Digest*. "The minuscule typeface has boosted my business by 67.1 percent," he writes.

Dr. Lemuel G. Zolf reports that the missing pages at the end of "Tracking Idaho's Mad Killer" in the October 1969 issue of *Morbid Detective* caused so much frustration among his patients that it diverted them from their normal fury when handed the bill for cleaning their teeth.

Ralph was so bucked by that response that he used the same technique with his article "Revealed at Last, the Real Killer of Warren G. Harding."

Ralph has his latest package almost ready for distribution next week and I can hardly wait. I'm told it contains an anniversary edition of Air Canada's *enRoute*, consisting entirely of old Claude Taylor columns from the back of the magazine.

I understand the people who run the Magazine Award ceremonies were planning to honour Ralph at the next function, but they were too late. The Canadian Medical Association beat them to it.

A MOVIE CRITIC'S RISE AND FALL

The recent premature death of once-popular film crit-ic Lindsey Tremaine calls to mind the circumstances that made him a household name before his descent to oblivion.

Few, I think, realize that Tremaine's fame was large-ly the work of former Hollywood boy wonder St. Clair Foncible Jr. Having pursued the record exhaustively, I am now able to reveal the details.

It may come as a surprise to learn that Tremaine was, at one time, the most vicious critic in the business. His brutal attacks on mainstream movies, especially Foncible's, were so notorious that he twice won the coveted Nasty Award for the most devastating review of the year.

"I'm tempted to dismiss the latest Foncible effusion, *Breakfast at Twilight,* as a simple abortion," he wrote. "But that would be a libel on those abortionists who have saved him from the consequences of many a romantic romp. Surely, Foncible, you must see that these ludicrous efforts to emulate the greats of the past will only cause your audiences to howl with laughter."

Tremaine's triumph was diluted, however, by Foncible's full-page ads: "A ROMANTIC ROMP ... YOU MUST SEE ... WILL CAUSE AUDIENCES TO HOWL WITH LAUGHER ... "—*Lindsey Tremaine, noted critic.*

The picture made so much money, it won six Oscars.

But when *Dinner at Dawn* was launched, Tremaine struck back: "Who does Foncible think he is—the porno king of Hollywood? Only a pervert would be attracted by the non-stop sex scenes, which I found revolting and inept. Who wants a succession of naked bodies writhing in bed? This incredible film will cause audiences to run, not walk, to the nearest exit of any theatre silly enough to screen it."

Foncible responded at once with billboards and full-page ads: "READ WHAT AMERICA'S TOP CRITIC SAYS OF *Dinner at Dawn:* "THIS INCREDIBLE FILM WILL CAUSE AUDIENCES TO RUN, NOT WALK TO THE NEAREST ... THEATRE ... NON-STOP SEX SCENES, BODIES WRITHING IN BED!"—*Lindsey Tremaine, internationally acclaimed critic.*

Internationally acclaimed! Tremaine's name was becoming a household word. Few actually read his reviews, which, like so many, were excessively long and tedious, and larded with words like "paradigm," "aesthetics," and "auteur"—which last sounded more like a three-wheeled foreign car than a Truffaut-style director. Conditioned by pithy *Reader's Digest* articles and TV sound bites, most moviegoers preferred to get their information in short, punchy, easy-to-read nibbles.

Foncible knew that. When Tremaine wrote that *Midnight Lunch* "might have been brilliant in less inept hands," Foncible seized "BRILLIANT—*Lindsey Tremaine*" for his ads. Only a handful of aesthetes caught on.

At one point, Tremaine tried to write a review that didn't contain a single word Foncible could exploit, even though he had to sacrifice his treasured literary style: "*Supper at Noon* is dumb! dumb! dumb! It is truly dreadful. It is awful. It is boring. It contains not one redeeming scene. A retarded school dropout could have done better. My advice to exhibitors. Keep it off the screen!"

Foncible immediately rented scores of billboards: "THE MOVIE AMERICA'S LEADING CRITIC DOESN'T WANT YOU TO SEE: *'Keep it off the screen!' says Lindsey Tremaine. So rush to your nearest theatre before the censors ban it and find out yourself why* Supper at Noon *needs censoring.*"

America's leading critic! It dawned on Tremaine that his real fame came from the quotes Foncible put in his ads. Surveys showed that scarcely anybody bothered to read his syndicated column. His 316 papers carried it because he was a Name; and he was a Name because Foncible had *made* him a Name.

And so he succumbed—subconsciously at first, then blatantly—sneaking in words and phrases he thought Foncible could exploit.

He began to praise Foncible's films for their "lineal

objectivity" and "tonal honesty," using such adjectives as "expeditious," "Fellini-esque," and "visually conceptual."

His handful of loyal readers loved his return to the old style, but Foncible didn't. To Tremaine's horror the ads stopped quoting him. He was no longer hailed as the country's leading critic. Eventually, the syndicate dropped him, and he died of a broken heart.

With Tremaine out of the ads, Foncible's films started to lose money and he was soon reduced to making kick-boxer movies in Hong Kong.

They needed each other, these two, like Dracula needed blood. They brought each other down. When one fell, the other toppled.

It was a symbiotic relationship, you might say.

STATION CHOO WITH THE SOUND THAT'S NEW

A proposal for a commercial radio station presented to the board of the Canadian Radio-television and Telecommunications Commission.

My radio station, ladies and gentlemen, will be a different kind of radio station. In fact, I intend to use that slogan: "Radio with a Difference." The difference will be that my radio station will be louder than the others.

The call letters of my radio station will be CHOO. This will allow the disc jockeys to go CHOO-CHOO-CHOO between every record and make railway sounds of various kinds, all loud. We will use the slogan: "The station with the New Sound." What will be the secret of the New Sound? Noise, that's what!

On Station CHOO with the Sound That's New we will pioneer a new concept of news coverage. We will have news every five minutes. A clever staff of rewrite men will reduce the most complicated stories to a single sentence, which will be rattled off at top speed by announcers who have been trained for weeks to hold pebbles on their tongues.

We will be First with the News at CHOO. More, we will bring you The News Before It Happens.

In case you think we are just skimming the cream off the news, let me reassure you that we will have Stories in Depth from CHOO's News Central. These incisive background stories designed to keep our listeners well informed and Abreast of the Facts will often last as long as thirty seconds and will be preceded by a fifteen-second fanfare on kettledrums.

Two features that I intend to introduce into my radio station in a radical move to grab the listening audience will be the constant repetition of the time and the weather. It will be our proud boast that CHOO listeners don't need a watch, simply a wrist radio. Indeed, in one of our contests, we will offer prizes to people who tear the watches off their wrists and mail them in to us. All proceeds will go to the Heart Fund, since we will be, above all, a Public Service Station.

The time will never be given straight: it will be sung by a pleasing chorus of sixty-four girls. Instead of an announcer simply saying "Six-fifteen," this chorus will sing, in sprightly fashion, "It has just reached a quarter past the hour of six, cha cha cha." The idea will catch on like wildfire, so don't leak it out until I get going.

The weather will also be sung. Actually, each weather announcement—and there will be ninety-six weather announcements daily—will consist of three songs. First, a trio will sing a little song announcing that the listeners are about to be told what the weather is. Then a forty-voice male chorus will sing the actual weather. This will be followed by a hillbilly duet who will sing another song explaining to the listeners that they have just heard a song about the weather. An announcer will then reveal when the next weather bulletin can be expected.

A good deal of attention will be given to velocities during these comprehensive weather reports, in the belief that the public is conducting a secret lottery on wind speeds. If the winds are nor'-nor'east at twelve, that intelligence will instantly be flashed to the listeners. Any change in the wind speeds will be analyzed by our own crack team of weather consultants.

I am also working on a plan to sing the news. This is a bit tricky as it will mean recording scores of anticipated news stories well in advance. It won't be so difficult, however, under our policy of reducing all news stories to eight-word bulletins. Weekend tragedies certainly can be recorded well ahead of the actual time: "The toll's mounting higher; four die in fire," for instance, subject to endless variations.

I have another idea up my sleeve which I think is going to be a real winner. My scheme is to hold a series of contests of various kinds by which certain lucky people can, if they phone CHOO's Contest Line immediately, get valuable prizes or money. For instance, at a prearranged moment we may suddenly announce that any man with blue eyes and bearing the middle name of Sacheverell who phones CHOO in the next forty-five seconds will receive a million dollars tax free. I'll concede that it may not be entertainment, but I'm gambling that it will get listeners.

Indeed, I suspect that CHOO will become the Most Listened-to Station by Actual Survey. It will also be First with the News by Actual Survey and the Most Loved Station by Actual Survey. These surveys will be handled by my own giant research organization, the Actual Survey Company, Inc., of Ottawa.

Let me dwell for a moment on our public service policy. I am going to develop the concept that public service is the lifeblood of private radio. Public service announcements of every kind will be given. We will, for instance, reveal where three out of thirteen of the police radar speed traps are to be found every day. At Christmastime we will warn all drivers constantly that they mustn't drink. All such announcements will be preceded by a quartet, which will sing a song to let the listeners know that a public service announcement is to be made. I also plan to enliven the waking hours of the very early morning with a Full Hour Festival of Public Service Announcements. Another First for CHOO, with the Sound for *You!*

Music on CHOO will be in the modern manner. I propose, however, to regulate the musical programming very stringently so that there will always be something for all. There will be, of course, only ten song hits played on CHOO in any one day. These will be the Top Ten, and each of them will be played once each hour or twenty-four times a day. Thus, our listeners can turn to CHOO at any hour of the day or night and be absolutely certain of hearing a Top Tune. Occasionally, for nostalgia's sake, we will reach into the past for an oldie. Sometimes we may even go back as far as 1992.

And that pretty well sums up my go-ahead policy for Radio with a Difference. Remember: Don't Feel Blue—Turn to CHOO.

The CRTC turned down this proposal on the grounds that there were, by actual count, some 112 similar radio stations already in operation across the land.

THE ART OF THE TV INTERVIEW

Grog Marvin, the internationally known star of stage, screen, and television, was in town recently taking part in some of those sincere-type modest TV interviews that have become as much of a ritual these days as a Kwakiutl puberty ceremony. Grog, following all the rules, remained painfully modest about his talents and gave all the credit for his success to his producer, his wife, his favourite dog, and other loyal assistants.

ELWOOD: Well, Grog, I hear you've completed a wonderful new picture, *I Was a Teenage Alien*.

GROG: That is right, Elwood, and I just want to say it was a real thrill working with that fine bunch of people at Tantamount. They're really a wonderful group of talent and any success the picture may have is due to their efforts, not mine.

ELWOOD: That's wonderful, Grog. Incidentally, I see you're one of the ten biggest box office names this year.

GROG: Yes, I've been very lucky, Elwood. I've had the good fortune to secure Manny Farber as my agent and Everson Goad as my director, without a shadow of a doubt two of the real geniuses of our business, and wonderful, sweet people in their own right. I give them all the credit, Elwood, not forgetting, of course, my wonderful wife, the beautiful and talented screen star in her own right, Murielle Marwood, who has always been a pillar of strength.

ELWOOD: That's wonderful, Grog. Incidentally, I see your newest record, *Rock, Rock, Baby,* has hit the million mark in sales. Congratulations, fella!

GROG: Don't congratulate me, Elwood. With a song as great as that, even a guy like me can't miss. And the wonderful thing is that the two kids who wrote it—Jackie-Lew Gronschell and Risible Green—not only have a great storehouse of talent but, in private life, they're a privilege to know as people.

ELWOOD: That's wonderful, Grog. Well, I see you're headed for Broadway next.

GROG: Yes, Elwood, I've been terribly lucky in securing the lead in what I think is one of the great dramas of our time, *Midnight at Dawn.* Fortunately I have a really great director in Randy del Regan, who did *Sunrise at Dusk.* If the play goes, it's he that deserves the credit, not me.

ELWOOD: That's wonderful, Grog. I hear you're making a war film soon.

GROG: You mean *The Blonde and the Bren Gun?*

ELWOOD: That's right—and I suppose the fact that you were one of the nation's most heavily decorated war heroes gives you some useful background, eh?

GROG: That's something I don't like to talk about, Elwood. I mean, it was my *men* who really won those medals—the ones that didn't come with the rations. I just happened to be around when they were passing them out ...

You can hear that kind of TV interview any day of the week. If only an international star of stage, screen, and TV would answer questions *this* way:

ELWOOD: Well, Grog, I hear you've just completed a wonderful new picture, *I Was a Teenage Jolson.*

GROG: That's right, Elwood—but let me tell you this: It's the last one I make for those idiots at Tantamount. I got absolutely no support, had to carry the entire acting burden myself. Personally, I think it's a real stink bomb, but if it makes a penny of profit, it will be no thanks to that crummy studio.

ELWOOD: That's wonderful, Grog. Incidentally, I see you're one of the ten biggest box office names this year.

GROG: That's right, Elwood, and I did it the hard way. I've always had lousy stories to work with and I've always had a rotten director. That Everson Goad, whose name was splashed all over the last one, ought to go to making porno movies. In this business, Elwood, you got to look out for Number One. If I hadn't played it that way I'd be a Big Nothing today. My agent is trying to steal me blind and all my wife thinks about is getting her name in lights. I'm packing her off to Reno.

ELWOOD: That's wonderful, Grog. Incidentally, I see your newest disc, *Rockin' on the Dock,* has hit the million mark in sales. Congratulations!

GROG: Don't congratulate me, Elwood. Congratulate those morons who buy that crud. Personally, I loathe rock music and I get down on my knees daily and thank the Lord above that I don't have to associate with those creeps who write what passes for a tune and lyrics. But it pays money, Elwood, and I like to live it up.

ELWOOD: That's wonderful, Grog. Well—I see you're headed for Broadway next.

GROG: Head for it maybe, but frankly I think we're going to die on the road with this dog. Whoever told Randy del Regan he was a director? If it comes off at all, it'll be because my name's up there on the marquee in big letters and I'm acting my fool head off with twenty years of experience behind me, while the rest of the company stands around with their fingers in their ears.

ELWOOD: That's wonderful, Grog. I hear you're making a war film soon.

GROG: You mean my new musical, *Hiroshima Serenade?*

ELWOOD: That's right—and I suppose the fact that you were one of the nation's most heavily decorated war heroes gives you some background, eh?

GROG: It gives me production values, boy, and I'm going to trade on 'em all I can. I mean, I figure the army owes me something besides a bunch of medals. After all, I didn't ask to fight the war; I was drafted.

ELWOOD: That's wonderful, Grog, and I just want to say a sincere thank you for coming on our show.

GROG: Whaddaya mean, thank you? Don't thank me, Dad—I mean, *pay* me!

SHAKESPEARE REVISES A PLAY

The scene takes place in the Globe Theatre, London, circa 1602. A production meeting is in session. Present are the executive producer, the director, the assistant director, the script editor, two beautiful and leggy script assistants, an agency rep, a public relations man, and a playwright, W. Shakespeare.

EXEC: Will, we think the script has tremendous possibilities. Basically, we like the story line.

SHAKESPEARE: (*Modestly*) I rather thought I'd made a ten strike with this one, Ed.

EXEC: Mind you, there are going to have to be revisions. I think we all agree it's short on production values.

SHAKESPEARE: (*Hotly*) Now hold on! I want you to get my basic concept here. This isn't another chase yarn like *Caesar*. There are subtleties of character here.

AGENCY REP: (*Sincerely*) Will, all of us think we have a really tremendous property here. Now don't get us wrong—it's just that, at the moment, it isn't—well, commercial. Now hear me out, Will—you got to admit the opening's slow.

SHAKESPEARE: That's just it! I wanted it slow! It starts slow and builds, see.

PRODUCER: You got to hook 'em fast these days, Will. You got to give 'em the old sockeroo right from the start. After all, this isn't 1591. Having the Prince find a letter telling him his old man was murdered ... I mean, that just doesn't swing, Will.

SCRIPT EDITOR: Look, Will, it's just a suggestion, but how about having the old boy's ghost pop up on the battlements and tell the kid how he was murdered?

SHAKESPEARE: A ghost? Are you cuckoo? Who'd swallow that kind of hokum?

EXEC: I like it! The surveys show the public goes for horror. Remember, Will, we helped salvage *Julius Caesar* with a ghost scene. Remember how they went for it in the gallery?

SHAKESPEARE: Yeah—and remember how the P.T.A. raised the roof? They said we were corrupting the young.

P.R. MAN: I think we can handle the P.T.A., Will, if you'd just write a moral little speech somewhere about the middle. Maybe have old Polonius tell his kid to be thrifty, never borrow money, that sort of stuff. Something they can use in the textbooks for memory work.

SHAKESPEARE: (*Groans.*)

SCRIPT EDITOR: It's a minor point, Ed, but I thought the recounting of the original murder lacked grue.

SHAKESPEARE: What's wrong with a knifing?

SCRIPT EDITOR: Nothing, but we overdid in *Caesar*. Suppose—now this is only a suggestion, Will—but suppose we have her kill him by pouring poison in his ear! It's never been done before.

SHAKESPEARE: (*Acidly*) Possibly because it's the silliest known method of bumping somebody off.

EXEC: Look, Will, would you go along with us just this once on this one? I think it has real possibilities. Try it our way, huh, Will? Okay, boy?

SHAKESPEARE: Oh, all right.

AGENCY REP: There's the teen angle to consider, Ed.

EXEC: Yes, we'd like your thinking on that, Will. The consensus here is that Ophelia ought to be a teenager.

SHAKESPEARE: Now, look! I let you commercial boys louse up *Romeo and Juliet* that way. Whoever heard of two fourteen-year-olds making love? Ophelia stays at thirty-two.

AGENCY REP: The surveys confirmed our thinking that other time, Will. The kids just have to identify. When she goes off her nut, they have to identify.

SHAKESPEARE: You're trying to survey me to death! I'm an artist, not a machine. I work on instincts.

EXEC: Go along with us on this, Will—just this once? It's an important segment of the market.

SHAKESPEARE: (*Shrugs.*) Well, you're paying the bills. Now what else have you got up your sleeves?

EXEC: (*Apologetically*) Well, the play is awfully short on sex. Oh, now I know what you're going to say! You're an artist! Okay, okay. We respect that, Will, and believe me, nobody here wants to interfere with the basic honesty of this play. But couldn't you just suggest a couple of things—like maybe the prince is secretly in love with his mother? That's always been surefire. He could get jealous thinking about her in bed with the guy who knocked off his old man. Just the odd innuendo, Will—in good taste, of course.

DIRECTOR: Chief, to be honest, I just can't see this ending. We've simply got to hype the ending.

SHAKESPEARE: You leave my ending alone. They walk out hand in hand into the sunset. It's sheer poetry.

EXEC: Now, now, Will, that's not the old Shakespeare talking. You know the public expects more than that from you. Let's face it—we've got to give them a blood bath.

PRODUCER: Yeah! Daggers, swords, a cup of poison maybe! The works!

DIRECTOR: Maybe have the prince leap into a grave at one point and dig up an old skull or something.

SCRIPT EDITOR: Hey! Have him *fight* in the grave. Boy, that'll knock 'em dead in the stalls.

DIRECTOR: (*Shouting*) Let's have him kill his girlfriend's brother!

PRODUCER: Surefire! And let's drown the girl. Suicide!

ASSISTANT: Crazy! And kill off the mother with poison!

PRODUCER: Kill off everybody! Use poisoned swords!

SHAKESPEARE: Stop! Stop! All you care about is sex and violence at the box office. You've got no appreciation of the artist. You louse up every play I write with your own vulgarities. I tell you there's going to be a reaction to this violence cycle in the theatre. There's a wave of Puritanism coming.

EXEC: Now, look, Shakespeare: this is a commercial enterprise and you better not forget it. I'm getting just a bit tired of your posturing about art. I, for one, don't intend to toss two years' investment down the drain just to humour your soul. I pay you to write commercial plays, and if you don't like it, there are plenty of others around who do. I had Johnson and Fletcher both in my office this morning. So you better blow with the combo, baby, or its Outsville for you.

SHAKESPEARE: All right. I know when I'm licked. Ten more years and I'm going to retire from this hack work to a place in Stratford where I can hold up my head in society.

P.R. MAN: There was one more point, Ed. The title?

EXEC: Yeah, the title's too long. We're going to call the show just plain *Hamlet*.

SHAKESPEARE: *Hamlet*? What kind of title is that? Whoever heard of *Hamlet*? It's a nothing title.

P.R. MAN: Maybe so, baby. But you got to admit it fits the marquees.

HOW WE CONVERTED OUR SPLIT-LEVEL INTO A MONSTER HOME

by Jed and Marcia Blair

(This article has been rejected by the following magazines: *House Beautiful, Better Homes and Gardens, Living, Sunset, Beautiful Homes,* and *Architectural Forum.*)

Then we first saw the advertisement in the paper we knew we simply had to have the house!

"Ultra-modern, brand-new, ranch-style bungalow," it read. "Finished in rubbed-down California redwood siding. Enormous picture window overlooks ravine lot. Modern built-ins and Scandinavian furniture. Open plan. Storage walls. Butterfly roof. A dream house, built for the future."

"Oh, darling," cried Marcia when she saw it nestling long and low against the ground. "It's just perfect! I can hardly wait to fix it up!"

"It will take months of hard work," Jed admonished. Yet secretly he was excited by the prospect and already planning ways to remove the enormous picture window and replace it with leaded panes. And so we bought it without further discussion. It wasn't much, but it was ours.

And yet, when on that first weekend we went out to commence the remodelling, we must admit our hearts sank. So much needed to be done; we hardly knew where to start. We decided finally to let the exterior go for the moment and get to work on the inside. Marcia enjoys rubbing down wood cabinets and she attacked these immediately while Jed went to work ripping out the wall-to-wall carpeting and replacing it with scatter rugs.

Marcia is wonderful with furniture. With a little sand-paper, some nails, and a sharp chisel, she can convert a Danish teakwood coffee table into the semblance of a golden-oak sideboard in a matter of hours.

Now, however, she turned her attention to the kitchen.

"The first thing to do is get rid of these hideous stain-less-steel cabinets," she said, with that amazing practi-cality of hers. "I know a little place where we can pick up some old cupboards and dressers for a song and maybe we can get a few dollars back on this metal from the junkyard."

After that, of course, it was necessary to strip off the Formica countertops (a friendly neighbour was happy to lend us his blowtorch) and get rid of the indirect lighting.

We really don't know what we'd have done if it hadn't been for our wonderful neighbours who rallied around one weekend for a real remodelling "bee." Without their help we don't think we could have removed those three stone planters that were cluttering up the living room.

Fortunately, one of our new friends happened to have a jackhammer. Reassembled in the garden, the planters made beautiful raised garden beds. We call it "bringing the indoors out," a phrase we think symbolizes our own philosophy of living.

One of the big problems we faced, and one which we had not really anticipated, was the total absence of room dividers, or "walls," as Marcia later christened them. The Living Area, which was cavernous, flowed into the Dining Area. The Dining Area flowed into the Food Preparation Area. The Food Preparation Area flowed into the Utility Area. The Utility Area flowed into the Family Area. The Family Area flowed into the Garden Area. And the Garden Area flowed right out the door.

"Look, Jed," Marcia exclaimed one day while she was helping lay flowered linoleum over the vinyl tile, "why don't we just close off all these different areas into separate cubicles and call them 'rooms'? That way we'd have complete privacy!"

It was a daring idea, but it made us the envy of the neighbourhood. Thanks to Marcia's idea of putting doors on everything, we were able to make each area a separate and distinct entity.

Then we turned our attention to the built-ins, and we spent several happy weekends tearing them out of the walls and replacing them with movable furniture. Old cupboards picked up cheaply at auctions, finely carved wardrobes in black oak, which Marcia purchased for a song at a little second-hand store on Yonge Street, and one immense roll-top desk in red maple, which kindly old Aunt Hattie just happened to have hidden away.

We quickly learned there's no use saving built-ins. We tried to sell them through the second-hand shops but they hardly realized the price of the cartage. In the end we simply chopped them up for kindling. We found the best way of dealing with storage walls—and here's a practical tip to you young homemakers—was simply to fill them with cement.

It's surprising how easily modern furniture can be converted to the familiar variety if you'll just absorb a little skill and patience. Sectional chesterfields should first be nailed and then sewn together into one piece. A set of good rockers does wonders for a modern Scandinavian chair. And we'll never forget that severe settee whose simple, uncluttered lines seemed to defy remodelling. Marcia, with some red-plum upholstery, a set of large buttons, and a few pounds of horsehair, did wonders with it.

Other tips: The best way to hide African mahogany, we found, is to cover it with a good brand of flowered wallpaper. Roses and forget-me-nots intertwined make a pleasing pattern, especially if they match your chintz slipcovers. A limed oak coffee table can easily be converted with sandpaper, elbow grease, and a good-quality dark-stain varnish. Incidentally, you'll be amazed and thrilled at the extra wall space when the old picture window finally goes out! We certainly were.

We actually moved into our remodelled home in late summer, though there was still plenty to be done. The exterior was a real mess! First, there was that long, low silhouette to be changed. We solved this by erecting a dummy roof with a steep gable over the existing one, so now we had an attractive Monster Home—one that matched the others on our street. A more difficult problem was the exterior siding. Have you ever tried to cover up polished California redwood? Believe me, white paint isn't the answer; we know because we tried it. What to do? Then Marcia had a flash of inspiration! Why not Insulbrick? It was easy to apply and now for the first time our new home really did fit in with the neighbours'.

HERBIE, THE SINGING NUTRIA:
A sixties fantasy

Once upon a time, up near Palgrave, there was a man named Bradley G. Framson, who owned a nutria farm.

For years he had dreamed of owning a nutria farm just as other men dream of owning a chicken farm.

He figured he could start with two nutria, a boy and a girl, and pretty soon end up with 5,596 nutria, which he would sell to make nutria coats, nutria wraps, nutria stoles, nutria muffs, nutria bras, etc.

Well, he *did* end up with 5,596 nutria, but the trouble was they were ordinary nutria, not mutant nutria, and the women were all wearing mutant nutria that year. He couldn't sell a single nutria.

So Bradley G. Framson decided he would have to shoot all 5,596 nutria and start from scratch.

However, by the time he bought a gun and several bullets he discovered that he had 11,192 nutria. So he decided it would be simpler just to shoot himself.

He went over to a quiet knoll overlooking a pleasant pond where the ducks skimmed across the water and the dragonflies hummed in the bulrushes and was just about to shoot himself when he heard a small, shrill voice singing "Beautiful Dreamer."

He looked around and there, to his surprise, was one of his nutria, singing away to itself.

"Why, hullo!" said Bradley G. Framson. "A singing nutria! My fortune is made! We will go to New York, sign up with a leading talent agent, cut several discs, and get on the David Letterman show."

So he picked up the nutria, whose name was Herbie, and boarded the plane for New York.

"Herbie," said Bradley G. Framson, "you and I are going to be rich and famous."

"Beautiful Dreamer, queen of my song," replied Herbie, in the key of E flat. *"Gone are the cares of life's busy throng."*

When they reached New York they went straight to the Broadway offices of Sam Frabnish, leading talent agent.

"What is it?" said the girl at the outer desk.

"A singing nutria," said Bradley G. Framson.

"Tuesday," said the girl. "That's when Mr. Frabnish sees the animal acts."

So they came back on Tuesday at two, and at four twenty-five they got in to see Mr. Frabnish. A gorilla was just leaving and he tried to eat Herbie on the way out, but Herbie was too fast for him.

"Sounds of rude world heard in the day; Lull'd by the moonlight have all passed a-way!" sang Herbie.

"What you got here?" asked Mr. Frabnish.

"A singing nutria," said Bradley G. Framson.

"Just one?"

"Of course, just one! What do you want, a chorus?"

"Choruses are dead," said Mr. Frabnish. "We had a bunch of chipmunks here a while back and they couldn't even sing. But singles are a dime a dozen. It's trios we want. You get me a trio of singing nutrias and I'll put your name in lights. But a single animal act don't go."

He ushered them to the door.

"I don't suppose he plays the mouth organ?" Mr. Frabnish asked as they left, and Bradley G. Framson shook his head sadly.

"Too bad," said Mr. Frabnish.

So Bradley G. Framson and Herbie the singing nutria went to another agent, named Moe Frabstor.

"A singing nutria," said Bradley G. Framson.

"Let's hear him sing."

So Herbie sang:

> *Beautiful dreamer, out on the sea*
> *Mermaids are chanting the wild lorelei*
> *Over the streamlet, vapours are born*
> *Waiting to fade at the bright coming morn.*

"Hold it!" said Mr. Frabstor. "The song has no beat and the words are corny. The kids want rhythm today. Get him to sing something with a beat."

"It's all he knows," Bradley G. Framson explained.

"But it ain't even on the Top Fifty," said Mr. Frabstor. "Besides, what would he do for the flip side? Sorry, I can't book him."

So Herbie the singing nutria and Bradley G. Framson went to see a third theatrical agent, whose name was Sid Farbfarsh.

"What you got there?" Mr. Farbfarsh asked.

"A real live singing nutria," said Bradley G. Framson.

"*List while I woo thee with soft melody,*" said Herbie.

Mr. Farbfarsh sat down heavily at his desk and clapped a slim hand to his brow. "Another one!" he cried, addressing the wall. "Why do they all come to me? *Why?* First it was chipmunks, then singing squirrels. At Christmas, singing reindeer, even!

"Look," he said to Bradley G. Framson. "These singing rodents are a dime a dozen. The gimmick has been overworked. Take my advice and put the nutria in some other line of work."

"But this is the only singing nutria in the world!" cried Bradley G. Framson.

"So who cares?" said Mr. Farbfarsh. "Look, kid, lemme give you a little bit of advice. There are the lights of Broadway down below winking up at us. And down there among those lights are the greats of show business who made good on the Great White Way. Each one of them had something—something unique.

"Now, I don't like to discourage you, but you got to have more than mere talent to claw your way up the ladder of success. You've got to have that certain, mysterious, electric 'something'—that *je ne sais quoi* to which we in the theatre give the name 'personality.' Y'unnerstan' me?"

Bradley G. Framson and Herbie the singing nutria looked down at the lights on Broadway and realized they just hadn't got it. So they went home sadly.

Fortunately for Bradley G. Framson, things turned out all right because when he got back home he discovered that styles had changed. Mutant nutria was out. Genuine original nutria was in.

So he sold all his nutria and made a million dollars and married the beautiful daughter of Conrad Faversham, the fabulously wealthy millionaire.

Maybe you saw her picture on the social pages a couple of days ago wearing her new high-quality muff, a wedding gift from her husband.

The muff, in case you're interested, was Herbie.

THE DARLING OF THE TALK SHOWS

Is there a more intriguing subject than clairvoyance? Almost everybody knows somebody who has had a clairvoyant experience. They have a dream in which their second cousin drowns in a well and sure as shooting it's proved that, at that exact moment, their second cousin did drown in a well. Or they have a premonition that a train is going to crash with their mother-in-law aboard and, by george, the train does crash with their mother-in-law aboard.

This proves that some people can see into the future, and it also more or less proves that there are such things as ghosts, flying saucers, seers, and so on. There are hundreds of instances, so it must be so.

Take the extraordinary case, for example, of Mrs. Charlie Golightly, the darling of the TV talk shows, who has been written up time and time again (she was on Sally Jessy Raphael just the other day). If that doesn't prove my point, then I don't know what I'm talking about. Mrs. Golightly actually *saw into the future;* there's no other explanation for it. It was a kind of mental telepathy or something.

Of course those who know Charlie Golightly and his missus intimately could have revealed her clairvoyance long ago. Talk about premonitions and dreams! Why, when she was only seven she had the strangest dream in which she saw her brother Dan horribly injured under a steamroller. The dream was just as clear as day, she said, and when she told her mother you'd have thought the old lady would throw a fit. Everybody was pretty relieved when Dan came home from school without a scratch. Fortunately for Dan there weren't any steamrollers in town or within fifty miles of town, but everybody agreed that he'd had a narrow escape.

Then there was that awful moment at the West Coronary Women's Institute Junior Tea when Mrs. Charlie (who, of course, wasn't Mrs. Charlie at the time, being only sixteen years old) suddenly stood up and shrieked that her aunt Agatha, in Sacramento, was dying at that very instant. It came to her like a cold knife in her heart, she said, and, of course, that pretty well broke up the social period that followed the flower-arrangement discussion.

Everybody said how it was amazing that a mere slip of a girl could sense what was happening thousands of miles away. Then everybody told stories about people they knew who had similar experiences with dying relatives. It was a miracle that Aunt Agatha lived for another three months after that, especially with her known heart condition.

After she was married to Charlie, Mrs. Golightly's dreams and premonitions grew more frequent, as all her friends know. This was especially true when Charlie, who is in leather and felt, started travelling by air to sales conferences. He had some narrow escapes, I can tell you; I never saw a man live so dangerously.

There was that time Mrs. Charlie woke screaming in the middle of the night; she had dreamed that the 707 to Miami had plunged into the gulf with all aboard. That was a close one. We had a sort of reprieve party for Charlie, who had been on that flight, when he returned safely.

Another time Mrs. Charlie had one of her premonitions and persuaded Charlie not to take the direct flight to L.A. She knew something terrible was going to happen, so Charlie took the train to Chicago and boarded another plane to L.A. It sobered us all to learn that the same jet he might have taken had been delayed *two hours*. No telling what might have happened if Charlie had been on it.

There were some other narrow escapes that really shook us all up. You remember when that big jet went off the runway at La Guardia? Mrs. Charlie pointed out to all of us that Charlie might easily have been on it if he had moved to the head office in New York three years previously, since it was known that a lot of head-office people flew regularly out of La Guardia. She had had a premonition that something terrible would happen if Charlie moved, so they had stayed put. Well, sir, that was a close one.

And then there was that big head-on collision over

the Grand Canyon. Charlie barely missed being on one of those planes. As Mrs. Golightly pointed out later, it was more or less on a direct line to Los Angeles and Charlie often went to Los Angeles—at least once or twice a year—and might have gone that week, or certainly that month if she hadn't had this absolutely vivid dream about seeing him dead with blood all over him.

Of course, it finally caught up with Charlie, as everybody knows. Mrs. Golightly has this terrible premonition that something was going to happen to Charlie on August 3, so she persuaded him to put off his New York trip for a week and stay home safely and, of course, Charlie did absolutely what she suggested. Fortunately for him, and for everybody else, nothing at all happened on August 3. I guess it was this that lulled him into a false sense of security. He took a plane to New York on August 10 at 10 p.m., and around 3 a.m. Mrs. Golightly woke screaming that she had had a terrible dream in which Charlie had been killed in an air crash.

Actually he got a little loaded, slipped on the top rung of the stairs at Kennedy Airport, and broke his neck, but as she explained to Donahue, it came to much the same thing. The newspapers were full of it, of course, especially when Mrs. Golightly told them about her dreams.

Everybody agreed that she had special powers, especially the newspapers. "Local Woman 'Dreams' Hubby's Death" was the way the *National Enquirer* put it. The story that followed explained how at the exact instant of the accident, Mrs. Golightly awoke from a dream in which she saw her dear husband lying at the bottom of the Kennedy stairs. The Psychical Research Society sent experts just to interview her, and for weeks the press was filled with occult experiences. Mrs. Golightly appeared on the Oprah Winfrey show, the Geraldo show, and *twice* on Larry King.

The story was written up in the *Reader's Digest* and several other magazines as one of those weird manifestations for which there is absolutely no logical explanation. Later, Mrs. Golightly was sent to Duke University for tests in extrasensory perception. She's had a couple of dozen dandy premonitions since then, but they haven't been written up yet.

As a result of all this, a good many once-sceptical people are now prepared to believe that there are those among us who really are psychic. How else can you explain experiences like Mrs. Charlie Golightly's? Don't tell me such things don't exist. We saw it on TV, didn't we?

WHATEVER BECAME OF WHOSIT?

Whatever became of Arthur Sproule? He was, you may remember, the greatest reporter of his day—foreign correspondent, investigative journalist, brilliant stylist. He was the recipient of so many awards that Who's Who needed a special section just to list them. He covered everything: terrorist attacks, holocausts, earthquakes, typhoons, and hurricanes. Whenever disaster struck, Sproule was there, giving the human side of the news.

That, in the end, was his downfall. When a devastating hailstorm destroyed $3.5 million worth of crops in the southwest corner of Saskatchewan, Sproule was dispatched by helicopter to cover the tragedy. He wrote graphically of the hailstones that thundered down from the heavens wiping out entire farms and destroying livestock. But when his copy poured into his newspaper's office, the city editor turned pale.

Sproule had neglected to use the standard description, that is mandatory in such stories. Where was the line *hailstones as big as golf balls?*

It wasn't there.

Sproule was hauled before the Press Council and subjected to disciplinary action. He did not attempt to defend himself. "At least," said the chairman, "you might have written: *hailstones as big as hen's eggs.* That would probably have been acceptable."

As a result, Sproule's paper took him off big disaster stories and confined him to writing obituaries. And here, once again, he blotted his copy book.

When the mayor died of terminal cancer after six weeks in a coma, Sproule was assigned the story. A hush fell over the editorial room when the city editor read what he had written, or, more to the point, what he hadn't written.

He *didn't* write that the mayor had succumbed *after a long battle with cancer.* He just said he died. For Sproule that was the end; he had broken one of journalism's cardinal rules—that nobody dies of cancer without a "long battle." Sproule was last heard of writing advertising copy for the Franklin Mint.

Whatever became of Jay Lassiter? In his day he was the country's greatest disc jockey. Everybody listened to his nightly program on radio station CHOO, perhaps because nobody could guess what he was going to play next. Indeed, he is generally credited with inventing the term "Golden Oldie" for numbers more than three years old.

His ratings soared until one night he made a dreadful gaffe. He introduced a Golden Oldie, "Stardust," which, he told his listeners, was one of his favourite numbers. "And here it is, friends and neighbours of radio land," he said, "Stardust."

In the booth there was a drawing in of breath followed by a stunned silence. Migawd! Had they heard right? Lassiter had *not* referred to the number as *Hoagie Carmichael's Immortal 'Stardust'!* The shame was too much for him to bear. He left town and was last heard of playing stride piano in a Yellowknife bar.

Whatever became of Marvin Kostelich? His name was unknown before the scandal that brought about his downfall. But in Washington and Hollywood, politicians and movie stars genuflected before him. Marvin Kostelich was, simply, the greatest ghost writer in history.

Everybody from congressional candidates to presidential hopefuls fought—and paid for—his services. He was the master of the well-turned phrase, the strident call to arms. But his second-greatest asset was his own carefully orchestrated self-effacement. And a few insiders knew that the words they heard from the political rostrum were actually Kostelich's words and not those of the leading politicians of the day.

It was at Oscar time that Marvin really shone. Famous movie stars pleaded with him to write the brief, pithy acceptance speeches that have become such a feature of the Academy Awards. Even those who were nominated but didn't expect to win beat a path to Marvin's door offering to pay big money for a few well-chosen words, just in case their name was drawn from the envelope.

The high point came when Sultra Lamarr, the odds-on favourite to win the Best Actress Award, managed to snag Marvin to compose her speech. "You know I'm no good at these things," she told him. "I can't put two words together. You do it for me and I'll pay any price."

Marvin named the price, which we will not reveal here, and wrote the speech for Sultra.

"I would like to thank," she began (reading his words off the TelePrompTer), "the academy for this wonderful award. I would also like to thank my wonderful agent, Manny Goldstein, for bringing me the property, and my wonderful director, Chase O'Brien, for doing what no other director could have done. I would like to thank my wonderful co-stars, Brick Ryan and Celeste Shalimar, for their support, and I would like to thank my wonderful parents for standing by me through thick and thin, and finally I would like to thank God for giving me this God-given talent."

These words brought tears to the eyes of many hardened members of the movie colony, while those in the know nodded to each other and whispered that Marvin had "done it again." One well-known director was heard to remark that Marvin's words, as read by Sultra Lamarr, were "sheer poetry." A few in the audience sensed trouble. What did she mean "finally"? Surely there was more.

The audience waited. Sultra paused, picked up the Oscar, and then, to a gasp of horror, left the platform.

An angry buzz rippled across the theatre and one or

two cries of "Shame!" were heard. *Sultra Lamarr had failed to thank her children!* It is true that Nikki, five, Marlon, three, and little Angelina, just one and a half, were the offspring of three different husbands, all of whom had obtained custody following a series of steamy court battles. That didn't matter. Since the early nineties, when recipients began thanking their children, in addition to their parents, it had become standard practice.

Sultra Lamarr was vilified for her gaffe until she revealed that the real perpetrator was the famous ghost writer Marvin Kostelich. Her career declined from that moment on. As for Marvin, he was through. He is now a rewrite man on the Fremington, Mass. *Courier-Star-Post-Record*. Sultra Lamarr occasionally appears in small-town summer stock. This month it's Agatha Christie's *The Mousetrap*. She plays the detective.

Whatever became of Susan Urbane? You remember her —the freckled kid with the pert hairdo? She was a kind of latter-day TV sob sister who was always sent out to get the human story behind some personal tragedy—a mother's reaction to her son's death by overdose, a family's response to the tornado that wiped out their home, that kind of thing.

One day Susan was sent out to cover a triple murder-suicide and to interview the sole survivor, a Mrs. Liz Fenwick, who had stood by while her daughter and grandchild were axed to death by her drug-addict husband. The cameras rolled as Susan tackled Mrs. Fenwick on the front porch of her home. But instead of asking the mandatory opening question (laid down in the CBC

News and Public Affairs rulebook), she simply put her arm around the weeping mother, expressed her condolences, and asked if she'd like a cup of tea.

Consternation! Had Urbane gone mad? She knew the drill; she was a professional. Yet at no time did she ask the regulation "How do you feel, Mrs. Fenwick?" question. Three members of her family were brutally murdered, their mutilated corpses lying on the front lawn covered by paisley shawls, and the hottest interviewer on the network failed to ask the survivor how she felt!

Today, Susan Urbane hosts a senior citizens' program on station CHOW in Wolverine Point, Alberta. She doesn't need to ask them how they feel; they all feel lousy and say so.

Five

DOCUMENTS
OF THE DAY

The historian, essentially, wants more
documents than he can really use;
the dramatist wants more liberties
than he can really take.
Henry James

HOLLYWOOD'S NEW RULES FOR CAR CHASES

Since every major film now released by Hollywood contains an obligatory car chase, the Academy of Motion Picture Arts and Sciences has felt it necessary to lay down a set of regulations for independent film producers.

USE OF POLICE CARS

1. During a police car chase, the police are to be shown as dangerous incompetents. Each film must use a minimum of seven cars (the median number is twelve), all of which are to be destroyed as the result of police stupidity and bad driving.
2. At least one pursuing police car must skid off the highway and roll down the bank into a shallow pond. Wet policemen emerging from the car must wave their fists and make other futile gestures.
3. When chased by a patrol car on a hilly, winding high-

way, the fugitive car should avoid one of the hairpin turns by plunging straight down the slope to make a perfect four-tire landing. The patrol car will attempt to follow suit but will turn end over end and burst into flames.

4. Every film should contain a four-stop crossroads. Four police cars involved in the chase must reach the crossroads from all four directions at the same time and bang into each other.

POINTS OF INTEREST

1. *Four-Lane highways*. All chases on four-lane highways will take place in the wrong lane with both pursuer and pursued trying to avoid oncoming cars. A minimum of eight cars (median eleven) will be knocked sideways off the highway.

2. *San Francisco*. Wherever possible, car chases are to be held in downtown San Francisco to take advantage of the hilly streets and to allow both pursuer and pursued to leap high into the air whenever a hill is encountered.

3. *Italian fruit markets*. All major chase routes must include a narrow lane lined with fruit carts. The Italian vendors will wear big moustaches and funny organ-grinder hats. The lead car will knock over one cart, scattering bananas and peaches. At that point an Italian will wave his fist and scream imprecations. The pursuing cars will knock down all other fruit carts as well as the screaming Italians.

4. *Parking garages*. Each chase will at some point enter

a parking garage and squeal around the tight turns, knocking other cars out of the way. A minimum of eleven parked cars are to be destroyed during the chase.

5. *Car ferries*. Every fleeing car will attempt to reach a car ferry. As the ferry leaves the dock, the fugitive car will leap the gap and land on the deck of the ferry. The pursuing patrol car will attempt the same feat and plunge instead into the water. A wet policeman will emerge, shout imprecations, and wave his fist at the ferry.

6. *Storefronts*. All storefronts along the line of the chase will be equipped with large plate-glass windows. Police cars that fail to make a tight turn will skid into other police cars, which will hit parked cars, hurling them through the plate glass windows of (a) soda fountains, (b) ladies' hair-dressing parlours, (c) supermarkets.

INNOCENT BYSTANDERS

1. While travelling the wrong way down a superhighway, the chase cars will carom off other cars driven by innocent bystanders who will be forced off the highway to crash into lamp standards, the concrete median, or other innocent bystanders.

2. A runaway perambulator with a baby inside will be involved in all major car chases. In spite of several near misses, both baby and carriage will emerge unhurt with the baby chortling and gooing in high good spirits.

3. In certain designated cases, the back seat of the car being chased will be occupied, unknowingly, by an innocent bystander. These include:
   - (a) A drunk who has climbed into the back seat to sleep it off and is convinced he is still drunk.
   - (b) The driver's mother-in-law, who was on her way to the beauty parlour when the chase began and who now proceeds to berate the driver, urging him to slow down and whacking him periodically with her umbrella.
   - (c) A young man and his blonde fiancée who climbed into the back seat in search of privacy and now cling to each other suggestively as the chase roars on.
   - (d) A bad guy who hugs the roof of the car and peers upside down through the windshield as the driver does his best to shake him off into the road.
4. At the height of the chase, a pair of elderly men will be seated on the sidelines engaged in a game of chess. Two cars will explode, another will be knocked out by gunfire, two handy fruit carts will be demolished. During this entire period both men will remain engrossed in their game, oblivious to all around them, saying nothing to each other except the one word: "Check!"

GUN PLAY

Every chase must be accompanied by gun play. When bad guys are involved they will fire torrents of bullets from half a dozen Uzis at the fleeing car. None of these bullets will do any damage. At that point the hero driver, using the rearview mirror as a guide, will fire a single shot from his Smith and Wesson, causing the pursuing car to skid off the road and burst into flames.

NOTE: These rules can easily be adapted for chases involving: (a) motorcycles, (b) bicycles, (c) roller-skates. Chases involving tracked vehicles require different rules, which will appear in our next bulletin.

A CATALOGUE OF REALISTIC CHRISTMAS TOYS

Realism and authenticity will be the continuing pattern of Christmas toys this Yuletide, toy manufacturers revealed today. More emphasis than ever will be put on making children's toys into miniature-scale copies— working models, in effect—of things to be found in the adult world. Thus toys will not only be "fun"; they will also be educational and instructive for they will encourage children to emulate their adult counterparts.
—Twentieth-century news item

REALISTIC MINIATURE SUBMARINE. *Does Everything a Real Sub Will Do!* Kids will go wild about this little item, which is just the thing for summer lake use. Made to actual Japanese specifications and based on similar midget subs used against Pearl Harbor during World War II, the ingenious device will remain under water for six hours before occupant strangles for lack of air. Emergency oxygen tanks allow extra half hour beneath surface. Actual torpedo tubes provide authentic effect and allow kiddies plenty of sporting fun attacking real-life targets such as pleasure boats, inflatable toys, skin-divers, and battleships. Sturdy aluminum finish and reinforced hull makes submarine 80 percent resistant to pressures up to six fathoms. Powerful diesel motor dives submarine at eight knots below surface, twenty-two knots surfaced. Forward gun smashes shore targets in believable manner up to 300 yards. Here's a Christmas gift that every red-blooded boy will want under the tree. Years of fun and summer-time pleasure at economy prices. Easy to assemble.

061-B232W (LARGE).....................................$762.46
11-J-134 TORPEDOES LOADED (pair)........$ 56.72
015-JJ2 EXTRA OXYGEN...........................$ 11.12
R23-B-57 COMPREHENSIVE
INSURANCE POLICY...................................$192.87

AT LAST! FROM AFRICA! THE FAMOUS "LIVING DOLL." *The Doll that actually Grows and Bleeds!* This is the doll you've read about in *Life* magazine. It not only wets and cries—it also grows inch by inch, year by year, and when jabbed at with a knife or other instrument, real blood flows and doll utters plaintive cries. Brought from wild African pygmy country (in chains), doll is amazingly lifelike. Takes bottle naturally, also takes tinned meat and other "goodies." It will provide hours of instructive fun for any child who wants something different. Child can test a milk "formula" on doll, which, if kept carefully, will grow real beard and be the talk of the neighbourhood.

10-C-231 (5 YEARS) $49.49
10-C-232 (10 YEARS) $59.59
10-C-233 (21 YEARS) $69.69

BOYS' THERMONUCLEAR DEVICE. Here's the very gift for younger boys who aren't ready for teenage pursuits and want something to keep them "busy." Instructive and educational, it is also fun for youngsters who will enjoy scale-model mushroom cloud, faithful in every detail to one that wiped out Hiroshima (cloud contains actual radiation up to 347 Roentgens). Device, when exploded, produces realistic "bang!" which delights the little ones as well as devastating 2.3 acres of built-up property. Let your youngster learn the principles of nuclear fission the do-it-yourself way while enjoying

himself either indoors or in the open country. Thermonuclear kit comes complete with Geiger counter to
measure radiation hazard following explosion. A real
hit with the younger kiddies.
2J-33B-017. Price delivered.............................$33.42

CHILD'S RADIATION SUIT. Useful when
handling thermonuclear device (above)
especially after fallout stage, it does double duty as a real fallout suit in case of
atomic attack. Keep America Strong (and
Canada, too, at a slightly higher price).
Equip your kiddies with these cunningly designed suits and help preserve the
younger generation for the future.
Kiddies will love struggling into these
clever one-piece garments. Solid-lead
boots are especially useful in develop-
ing young muscles. Navy, Brown, Gray, and Plaid. Sizes
3, 4, 5, 6, 6x.
10-B6172. Price delivered $14.98

REAL MINK COATS, WRAPS, AND STOLES FOR LITTLE
GIRLS. Here's the answer to the prayers of any eight-
year-old tot who wants to learn how to "keep up with
the Joneses"! Here's your chance to make your child
the absolute envy of the neighbourhood with a genuine
expensive mink. For the sake of the kiddies we've
stamped the price right into the lining for easy reference.
If your child has been "neglected" by the rest of the
neighbourhood, if she's the "ugly duckling" of your

street, or the wallflower of the local Girl Guide or Explorer group, these mink offerings, cut to the latest Paris styles, are the answer to a mother's prayer. How the other children will turn green with envy when she parades up and down on Christmas Day, literally "dripping" with mink! Be the first in your block to buy your little girl Real Mink.

X-224-3J Stoles from...................$1,024.44
X-225-3J Wraps from..................$1,572.22
X-227-3J Coats from....................$8,776.21

DIVORCE IN OUR TIME:
A modest proposal

The following paper has been prepared for presentation to the Anglican Synod of the Archdiocese of Toronto. Copies have been sent to the Moderator of the United Church of Canada, and also the Presbyterian Church in the hope that decisive ecumenical action will follow.

It is not too much to say that divorce in our century has not only become fashionable, it has also become the norm. Yet all these split-ups are handled untidily, without pomp or circumstance, so that much of the time we do not know which of our friends were divorced last week. Or we hear that they are getting divorced, but we have no way of discovering when the divorce occurs. Sometimes they do not get divorced after all and refuse to speak to those of us who have told our friends that they've split.

The problem is that no proper ritual, no sensible code

of behaviour, exists for people getting divorced as for people getting married. Why not? Why shouldn't there be a divorce ceremony laid down in the Book of Common Prayer? The idea has considerable merit and should appeal to florists, department stores, telegraph offices, social editors, caterers, and Syd Silver's Tuxedo Rentals. Formalize divorces as we formalize weddings, I say! Send out engraved invitations in double envelopes. Invite your friends and enemies.

The ritual, in my opinion, should be held in church and it ought to be presided over, whenever possible, by the same minister who forged the original bonds of matrimony. We will have ushers, of course, wearing white carnations in their buttonholes and conducting friends of the husband and friends of the wife down the aisle, and seating them balefully on opposite sides. (You'll remember that she never could abide his friends.)

The divorce itself will have been handled by the new divorce-counselling service of the T. Eaton Company. There may be a bit of trouble over that. At one point *he* swore that if he had to wear formal clothes there wouldn't be a divorce, and *she* went off and had a good cry and said she just couldn't go through with it, there were too many details. But finally they patched it up and here he is, entering from a side door with the Worst Man (sometimes known as the Other Man). It is the job of the Worst Man to snatch the wedding ring from the little woman's hand at the appropriate moment and to fling it on the floor and stamp on it.

Now the church doors swing open and the wife comes down the aisle on the arm of her father who once gave her away and is now, somewhat reluctantly, taking her back. The bridal procession may also include a Matron of Honour (sometimes known as the Other Woman) and several flower girls (the children of the divorced couple, whose custody is still in doubt).

The ceremony itself should be simple and dignified. As few simple "I do's" in answer to the minister's question as to whether he or she rejects him or her as each other's wedded spouse, never again to have, hold, love, or cherish. Then the usual rhetorical remark: "If any here present know cause as to why these two should not be separated, ye are to declare it." It is to be hoped that there will be no sloppy speeches at this point and that the ceremony can continue with dispatch.

Time now for the newly divorced couple to go into the vestry and scratch their names off the marriage register. Meanwhile, the local tenor sings some appropriate song such as "Brokenhearted." The department-store service includes photographers, not only for the social pages but also for the Divorce Albums that are mementoes of the occasion. A divorce, unlike a wedding, requires two photographers, for it will be traditional that the couple leave by two separate exits. The guests throw confetti and old shoes—those shoes that he was always leaving around the house, to her annoyance.

A reception follows and there is the usual receiving line, congratulations from friends, a mildly intoxicating punch, and, of course, a toast to the new divorcée by her mother, who says how glad she is that her little girl has finally got rid of that monster. The ex-groom replies with a few graceful remarks of his own about in-laws. Some

telegrams are read, mainly salutations from old girlfriends
to the ex-groom, inviting him up to the family's place for
a steak dinner on Saturday night.

And now we cut the cake, while the photographers
stand by. The two figures atop the divorce cake are, of
course, facing resolutely away from each other. There
may be a tendency for one or other of the happy pair to
want to slice the head off one of these little figures, but
this ought to be discouraged.

After the cake cutting (the guests each get a piece to
keep under their pillows), it's time for the little woman
to toss away her bouquet. All the young matrons vie for
it, because there's a charming legend going the rounds
that she who catches the flowers will be the next in line
at Reno.

Did I mention the wedding gifts? They're on display
in an adjoining room, each marked with the name of the
donor. That's right—they're giving them back. Some, I
fear (the vases, crockery, and the like), have become a
bit dented as a result of those hearty marital arguments
that led to the divorce.

The divorce ceremony is a bold step forward. There
is little doubt that some day it will be made compulsory
for commercial, if not religious, reasons. As a result,
thousands will be content to stay married rather than go
through another expensive ritual.

Face it: weddings have become so complicated that
scores of young people are already living without bene-
fit of clergy because they cannot face the six months of
planning that the modern white wedding demands. By
making divorce ceremonies compulsory, the church will

strike a blow for permanent relationships. Divorce ceremonies may be complicated rituals, but is anyone bold enough to say that they are more foolish than the ones we have now?

A CATALOGUE OF THE NEW LABOUR-SAVING DEVICES

Amazing new instrument actually *does away* with present clumsy dial or push-button systems. No more sore fingers, no more stupid touch-tone errors, thanks to the "Speaker Phone"! Simply lift receiver and *speak* your number into the Magic Mouthpiece. In a few moments your party will answer. It sounds incredible, but modern science has actually perfected the system so that most homes will soon be equipped with the dialless instrument. Radical new "upright" design places mouthpiece at actual mouth level. No stooping, squatting, bending, or neck craning needed. Be the first in your neighborhood to own one!

Now you can enjoy *indoors* the delights of charcoal-broiled meats, chicken, game, and spareribs, with this amazing cast-iron indoor barbecue. Built to last for years, the new device allows you to hold "rainy day" barbecue parties in the comfort of your home— yes, and even in winter! Don't let storms or unseasonable weather spoil your fun; invest 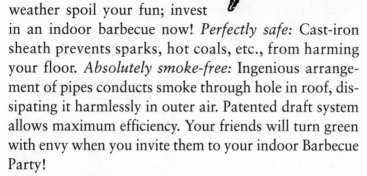 in an indoor barbecue now! *Perfectly safe:* Cast-iron sheath prevents sparks, hot coals, etc., from harming your floor. *Absolutely smoke-free:* Ingenious arrangement of pipes conducts smoke through hole in roof, dissipating it harmlessly in outer air. Patented draft system allows maximum efficiency. Your friends will turn green with envy when you invite them to your indoor Barbecue Party!

 Here's good news for housewives. Our new, ingenious freezer-refrigerator does away with defrosting-day blues, thanks to our new Custom Ice Delivery system, which takes the drudgery out of freezer care. Think of it! No more filling pans with water! No more waiting for ice cubes to freeze in trays! No more messy defrosting. Now *we bring the ice to you!* Yes, we actually deliver it to your door and place it in your refrigerator for as little as a few cents a week—

scarcely more than you'd pay in electrical charges with your old-fashioned fridge. And here's an added feature: Custom Fridge is completely sheathed in beautiful golden oak, especially designed to blend with modern panelled kitchens. Get rid of that "appliance look." Order a Custom Gold-Oak Freezer-Fridge today!

Now you can have good grooming for less money! Fresh shirts can be worn twice as long by eliminating soiled collars—and that's what this smart new shirt collar can do for you! You'll never look limp or ungroomed when you wear this beauty because with a simple push-pull, click-click action you can *change collars in an instant without removing your shirt!* And, best of all, the collar retains its shape at all times because it's made of pure celluloid! If you want to have that well-starched look, and at the same time save on laundry bills, then get rid of those old-fashioned soft-collar shirts and switch to the style that's sweeping the nation.

Here's an amazing new invention that will help you improve your writing skills. Now you can write with a firm, clear line that never skips, yet changes in width as you shape the letters. The line is stronger, clearer than that produced by old-fashioned ballpoint, thanks to a new patented stylus called a "nib." And here's an additional feature: you no longer need to replace cartridges. An ingenious sac within the pen contains a supply of writing fluid or "ink" which is sucked up by a simple filling action.

Ingenious new washing device is simplicity itself to operate—and fun, too! Guaranteed to contain no moving parts of any kind, it's the answer to the prayers of any housewife baffled by the intricacies of old-style

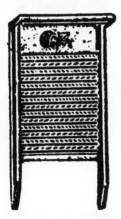

washers. Nothing whatsoever can go wrong with the new do-it-yourself washer! Ingenious glass "riffles" scrub clothes whiter that white before your eyes as you pass them across the face of this washer. And it's healthy exercise, recommended by leading doctors for overweights and shut-ins. Well-constructed and completely portable, it can be stored easily in a kitchen cupboard when not in use.

Bothered by persistent hydro failures? Then here's the modern invention you've been dreaming of. A completely wireless rug cleaner that does not depend on electrical contact for efficiency. The product of years of research, it is childishly simple to use! Simply move it briskly across your carpets, and *presto!*—the rotating miracle brushes do the rest! Move it to any room in the house without plugging it in; the rug cleaner will astonish you by continuing to operate without wire or cord. They said it couldn't be done—but here's proof that it can! Works even in houses that contain no electrical wiring.

A TREATISE ON TWENTIETH-CENTURY BEHAVIOUR

The following natural laws, arrived at after forty years of experiment and observation on carefully selected samples of respondents, are immutable and unchanging.

CHILDREN IN GROUPS

Law No. 1: In any group of six children or more under the age of eleven, there will always be one child crying.

Law No. 2: In any group of ten or more such children, there will always be two children crying.

Law No. 3: In any group of seventeen children of any age, there will always be a minimum of three children crying.

CHILDREN DRINKING MILK

Law No. 1: In any group of six children drinking milk,

there will be at least one glass spilled.

Law No. 2: In any group of ten children drinking milk, there will be three glasses spilled.

Law No. 3: In any group of seventeen children drinking milk, the container will be spilled and broken.

Law No. 4: Any child under the age of four will spill its milk even when in groups of one.

Law No. 5: Any child under the age of four who spills its milk will, when offered a second cup, invariably spill it again.

These laws apply equally to Freshie, Kool-Aid, soft drinks of all kinds.

CHILDREN'S BIRTHDAY PARTIES

Law No. 1: Any birthday party of more than seven male children under the age of eleven will invariably end in a fight.

Law No. 2: Any child's birthday party in which the number of guests exceeds the number of the actual age of the child for whom the party is being given will end in disaster.

CHILDREN'S CONCERTS AND RECITALS

Law No. 1: When more than six children appear in a concert or recital one will refuse to go on.

Law No. 2: When more than ten children appear in a

concert or a recital one will refuse to go on and two will burst into tears.

Law No. 3: Children's concerts scheduled to start at 8:15 p.m. sharp will invariably get under way at 8:52 p.m. sharp.

Law No. 4: Children's musical recitals advertised as being 90 minutes in duration will invariably run for 186 minutes and 27 seconds.

Law No. 5: A child scheduled to compete and/or perform at such a recital at 9:10 p.m. on the program will actually appear on stage at 9:52 p.m.

Law No. 6: In any group of twenty-seven children performing at a musical recital and/or concert there will be twenty-seven mothers.

Law No. 7: In any group of twenty-seven children performing at a musical recital and/or concert there will be three fathers.

Law No. 8: In any concert and/or musical recital in which the average performance of each child does not exceed six minutes and thirty-two seconds the average attendance time of each father will not exceed six minutes and thirty-two seconds.

ADULTS AT PARTIES

Law No. 1: If a party is scheduled to run from 4 to 7 p.m., then that party will run from 5:30 to 10 p.m.

Law No. 2: If twenty-two people are invited to a party

commencing at 9 p.m., one person will invariably turn up at 9 p.m.

Law No. 3: At any party lasting more than three hours and twenty-two minutes, at least one woman will be crying.

Law No. 4: At any party catering to more than ten people, at least two glasses will be broken.

Law No. 5: At any party catering to more than seventeen people, at least four glasses will be broken.

Law No. 6: At any afternoon party in which the guests stay until after midnight, all glasses will be broken.

Law No. 7: A wife who has had two drinks on being offered a third drink will decline it. She will then drink half of her husband's drink. She will then change her mind and say that she would like a third drink. Her husband will drink this drink.

Law No. 8: Exactly fourteen minutes and seventeen seconds after the host announces that there is nothing more to drink, all guests will leave, no matter what the hour is.

Law No. 9: In any group of seventeen adults taking part in a party and buffet there will be two husbands who absolutely refuse to eat.

WIVES AND PROMPTITUDE

Law No. 1: A wife arranging to meet a husband at a designated spot exactly at 6:15 p.m. will meet him at that spot at 7:01 p.m.

Law No. 2: Any wife who is more than seventeen minutes late for an appointment will have an iron-clad excuse.

Law No. 3: If a husband is waiting for a wife and leaves his post for more than seventeen seconds the wife will appear during that interval. She will invariably ask the husband why he is late.

VACATION BEHAVIOUR

Law No. 1: When leaving home by car for a two-week holiday, a family will drive an average of 6.3 miles before returning for forgotten luggage.

Law No. 2: On extended motor trips when there are six or more children and adults in a car, there will always be at least two children or adults crying.

Law No. 3: When staying overnight with friends, any family of four will leave behind enough clothing, toys, and miscellaneous incidentals to fill a cardboard container whose dimensions are 24" x 24" x 12".

Law No. 4: The size of such container will increase in direct proportion to the number of children and the length of the stay.

GARAGE BEHAVIOUR

Law No. 1: No matter how much time a garage is given to fix any make of automobile, that automobile will not be quite ready when the owner calls for it.

Law No. 2: If a garage says that a given automobile

will be ready in "about one more hour," that automobile will be ready in two hours and seventeen minutes.

Law No. 3: If a mechanic says "give me until tomorrow," give him until Tuesday unless it happens to be Monday.

Law No. 4: If a garage man estimates that a repair bill will come to "about $50.00," that repair bill will invariably come to $94.32.

These laws apply in essence to all types of repairmen.

A COFFEE LOVER'S CALL TO ARMS

Men of courage and good heart! The glorious moment has arrived! We small band of comrades, we happy few, have been chosen to lead the attack. Years from now our grandchildren will marvel at the story of this day. In small villages, those of us who survive, grown bent with age, will be pointed out as members of that gallant crew who on this day, which happens to be St. Crispin's Day, fought with honour against fearful odds.

For this is the day, my lads, when we launch our campaign to abolish instant coffee!

First, I wish to make it clear that every man who follows me does so of his own free will. If there be one so craven that he has no stomach for the task, let him speak up. He will be given a handsome pension at once, plus this fine fifty-seven piece set of genuine silver-plated tableware in the beautiful Carleton design, and will be free to return home with no questions asked. We do not wish such men with us on this glorious day. What? Nobody speaks? Stout fellows!

First, I shall ask the company sergeant-major to pass among you with mugs of real honest-to-goodness coffee to strengthen your resolve. The heartening brew is made from freshly ground beans and cold tap water, carefully smuggled in from a bootleg restaurant that still allows it on the menu. Whiff that pungent aroma! Savour the mellow, full-bodied flavour! Man, oh, man: that's coffee! Please put that phrase into the war diary, young Spalpeen; I have an idea it may become immortal.

Now, I know that each of you men harbours an implacable hatred for the foe. You have seen your wives, your children, your old family retainers slowly poisoned by that insidious concoction we are pledged to destroy. Friendships have been ruined, marriages wrecked, homes split asunder by that vile instant brew.

Oh, I can tell you tales, my stout lads, that will turn your hearts to stone and give your sword arms strength and send you into battle with the red mist of Revenge clouding your eyes.

Here, on my right, stands a pitiful wreck of a man, ruined by instant coffee. You knew him as Hereward Hardicanute, as stout a yeoman as ever drew longbow. I venture to say that no happier couple ever existed than Hereward and that buxom village lass to whom he was betrothed. Many a young swain's heart was broken when fair Gwyneth Groghart chose Hereward as her life's companion and other clichés.

Each morning, lads, before Hereward left for the office, his Gwyneth would, with her own mild-white hands, prepare him a steaming mug of real honest-to-goodness down-to-earth freshly brewed coffee—the kind we used to see portrayed in the slick-magazine advertisements of yore. And when he caught the streetcar home at night, it was with a song in his heart because he knew his Gwyneth would have another cup of mellow, richly satisfying, honest-to-goodness coffee waiting for him.

Then, one night, horror struck! Picture the scene of carnage: the percolator smashed and broken; the Silex wrecked; the air heavy with the stench of instant coffee! And there, slumped across the chesterfield, his beautiful Gwyneth. Yes, men, the child bride was no longer in the kitchen, carolling to herself as she measured out each level tablespoon. She was lolling at her ease, munching chocolates and reading *True Movie Romances,* while on a nearby table, like a brooding presence, there lurked that familiar bottle with the stars on top.

Worse was yet to come. It was not enough that Hereward was obliged to choke down the foul-tasting, lukewarm liquid. Soon he discovered his wife was actually serving it to her guests. Think of the shame, the humiliation! Shunned as pariahs by the entire village, the Hardicanutes couldn't even get up a table for backgammon. The very curs avoided them. It was the end of their relationship. Now this human husk stands before you—mute testimony to the forces of evil each of us has sworn a solemn oath to banish.

But before we yet press forward with our naked swords flashing in the sunlight and our blood-red banners rippling proudly in the breeze, etc., let me warn you of the pitfalls that lie before you.

Fair-tressed maidens will peer from the TV sets holding jars of instant coffee in their well-manicured hands and singing siren songs about aroma and flavour! Stuff your ears with cotton, which may be drawn as a company charge at Q.M. stores, and press on.

Beautifully tailored youths, with gleaming teeth and sincere smiles, will look up from coffee tables, smacking their lips and trying to win you over with sweet talk about flavour buds. List not. Raise, indeed, your far-shadowing spears from behind your richly dight shields and give it to them right in the gizzard.

Each of you knows his task. The whole plan has been gone over carefully on sand tables at squad level. The spearmen will go directly to the advertising agencies, looting, burning, and pillaging as they advance. Account executives will be seized as hostages; all others will be put to the sword.

Yeomen will advance in columns of threes upon the television and radio stations. All announcers mentioning instant coffee are to be garrotted at once, as are comedians inserting the phrase into their scripts for payola. Beautiful blonde demonstrators are to be ravished, as laid down in the syllabus of training. Network presidents are to be force-fed instant coffee until they strangle.

The light-machine-gun teams will cover the main assault on the factories, assisted by the three-inch mortar squads. The giant, evil-smelling vats where real honest-to-goodness coffee is boiled down into instant powder will be dynamited. Highly paid scientists, working on new methods of ruining coffee, will be shot on sight, along with their wives, children, and pet Cadillacs. Plant executives down to the rank of foreman will be boiled in their own coffee. Ordinary workers are to be spared, since they will have been forced to work in the factories against their wills. They will help lay the groundwork for the enlightened society we plan in the postwar period.

But enough of words! The time for action is at hand! Advance, bold sons of aegis-bearing Zeus. Our cause is just! We come as liberators of the oppressed! I have checked with the archbishop and he informs me that God is on our side! Death to instant coffee! On to victory!

A SUBTREASURY OF CLICHÉS FROM OUR ERA

Well, thank you for those very kind words, Ed. Believe me, this new post does represent a challenge for me, and all I can say is, I'm going to give it my very best. And whether or not I make good, I know that I'm going to have a lot of fun trying.

First, let me say, gentlemen, how very sorry the premier is that he is unable to be with you this evening. I know he would want me to express to you his very real regret that previous commitments have made it impossible for him to attend. I hope, in his absence, you will permit me to read this prepared speech.

What's happening to us, Marcia? In the old days, even when we lived on salami and chips, we seemed to be so close. And now, I don't know, it's as if we were drifting apart.

Well, Dick, I just want to thank you for taking time out from your busy schedule and coming down here to the studio to talk with us tonight, and I think I speak for all the boys and girls on the show when I say we wish you all the luck in the world, fella.

My warmest thanks to Miss May Fellows, Miss Alicia Whitehead, and Miss Freda Schon for typing the manuscript through successive drafts. A special word of gratitude, too, to Miss Aimee Larson for reading the proofs and making valuable editorial suggestions, and Miss Anne Sylvester for her encouragement throughout. I am also deeply grateful for the special help of Miss Patricia Lowe and Miss Abigail Sells. And finally, of course, my thanks to my dear wife, without whose patient understanding this book would not have been possible.

Try to understand, Mrs. Hargreaves: Jimmy didn't die in vain. Thanks to him, thousands of decent, God-fearing American boys will grow up to live useful and worthwhile lives without fear haunting their footsteps. Jimmy isn't really dead, Mrs. Hargreaves; not as long as America lives!

Before I commence my formal address this evening, gentlemen, I should be remiss if I did not thank your chairman for the very kind remarks addressed to myself. I can assure you he has been far too generous, and I am afraid after such a fulsome eulogy that what follows is apt to sound like an anticlimax!

DEAR AUNT MINNIE THANK YOU FOR THE LOVELY PAIR OF SOCKS THAT WERE JUST WHAT I WANTED HERBIE GAVE ME A BEAR THAT REELY RUNS BACKWARDS

I HOP YOU HAD A LOVELY CHRISTMAS LOVE YOUR LOVING NEPHEW JOE.

You got to listen to me, Jake! You're not going out on that street alone! Not after all the promises you made. Just this once, Jake, you got to hear me out. This isn't your fight. What do you want to get mixed up in it for?

I should like to turn now to another dilemma of our industrial civilization: this endless search for a will-o'-the-wisp called "security" which is stifling individual enterprise in this country. Where, I ask, is the rugged individualism of yesteryear? Would they have built this great nation to its present state of prosperity had they worried about something called "security"? The answer, gentlemen, does not lie in security, it lies in increased production.

What drives you, Johnny? What keeps you running? Have you ever stopped to ask yourself why you're running and what you're running from? Some day you're going to have to stop running, Johnny. Some day you're going to find out that a man can't keep running from himself.

Mr. Jackson and class: The subject of my speech to you this afternoon is "Our Community." Our community is, indeed, a fortunate one. Situated as it is between the teeming industrial centre of Lemmingville, and the richly endowed agricultural belt of the Wackensak Valley.

Mind you, gentlemen, I have nothing but respect for our trade unions. Over the years they have raised the status of the labouring man to a high peak, and I doubt that there is anyone in this vast audience tonight who would deny their intrinsic worth. And yet, one cannot escape the feeling that today union leaders are demanding too much.

We've always been peaceable folk, son, you know that. We never did hold with violence of any kind and we always brought you up to believe the Lord's way was the best way. But there comes a time when every man has to stand up for what he believes is right.

My only regret is that I am leaving all you girls behind, with whom I've spent so many rewarding moments. Whatever happens, I'll never forget the gang here at the office and I know I don't have to tell you that, as soon as we're settled, the latch is always open to each and every one of you, and I mean that sincerely.

I think I can say—and I believe I speak for every member here tonight—that seldom have we in this club heard as inspiring and as down-to-earth an address as our speaker of the evening has honoured us with.

Well, folks, I see the old clock on the wall is coming around once again to the sixty-minute mark so I guess that sorta kinda winds it up for another Friday night. It's been fun being with you: see you all next week at the very same time. Meanwhile, drive safely and take care, d'ya hear?

THE FINAL ABSURDITY

The definitive sentimental "lake" poem.
Margaret Atwood

MY LAKE

Memories come flocking back
Like errant sheep,
Memories seeded before real memory began;
Memories of a phantom lake, moonstruck,
And I in my crib, hard by the window,
Peeping through half-open shutters
Gurgling and cooing at the parental slap
Of the persistent waves caressing the shore.

Memories of childhood,
Of skinny-dipping in the cove beyong the cottage,
White buttocks flashing wetly in the sunlight.
(We marvel at the rough, male kiss of the sand
while filching quick, embarrassed glances at each
other's loins.)

Memories of youth ...
I, still a stripling,
Groping for Mavis in the canoe,
The mysterious globe of the moon
Illuminating her own twin globes,
Whiter than the moon herself —
I see them now,
Reflected in the shivering waters of the lake,
And I yearn for them still.
Ah, Mavis! After you came to me
I thought the lake itself —
My lake! — had moved beneath us
Before the canoe capsized.

My lake! the memory of its wetness
(For this lake was ever wet)
Soothed my fever in those distant climes
When I, ever the wanderer,
Roamed far from its shores,
Hunting the elusive *thork*
In the bush country of the *Graal*,
Or seeking the missing *khazibe* people
That luckless tribe whose members
They do say still cling to tenuous life
In the gnarled Mountains of the Lost.

The years have not been kind;
My step falters, my sight is blurred.
Only the lake endures,
I tell myself,
When, home at last,
I make one final pilgrimage to its shores.
Yet somehow it eludes me, my beautiful lake.
Why does it not beckon from beyond the trees —
Winking in the sunlight
Like an old, accommodating mistress?

Now, at the turn in the road,
Seated on a rustic bench
I spy a figure from the past.
Older than time he is,
Wizened, broken,
His nut-brown face creased like an old shirt.
Why, I cry out in delight, it's Old Tom!
He, too, endures.

He starts to rise, extending a gnarled hand.
Young Master Derek! You've come back
After all these years!
I motion him down, his knees creaking like a
Zamobzi *zhut*, riding at anchor.

I stare into those rheumy eyes
That have seen so much
And ask the question that haunts me:
Where is my lake, Old Tom?
What has happened?
He removes the ripened pipe from his yellow teeth,
Taps dottle from the bowl,
Croaks out an epitaph.
Gone! cries Old Tom. Gone!
Your lake is no more.
No more? My lake no more?
Oh, say not so ...
'Tis true, the old man whispers —
And, as he speaks, salt tears roll down his sunken cheeks
Like freshets from a mountain stream.
No more! says wise Old Tom.
It ain't a lake no more.

Meech—no longer a lake?
A cry of pain escapes me.
No longer a lake, repeats Old Tom.
No longer a lake:
Only a flawed public document.